CW01645679

FROM THE HEART

THE HEART LED WAY TO GET UNSTUCK, FIND YOUR PURPOSE AND LIVE YOUR PASSION

ALVINA MENZIES DR BHARTI RAJPUT
CLAUDIA ROMERO
DANIELLE GAFFNEY DU PLOOY GENNA DELANEY
JEN CADGER KIRSTY J MCLEAN
MICHELLE DE ALMEIDA RADKA TELYCKOVA
RENATA TARI VICKI OSTROWSKI

INSPIRED WORLD PUBLISHING

INTRODUCTION

ALVINA MENZIES

First and foremost, I would really love for you to take a moment to pause, to recognise the amazing women who will share their stories "From The Heart" with you through this book. I feel very privileged to have had the opportunity to hold space for them over the last few months, to help build their trust and confidence in their own ability to become published authors, a community of wise, successful women preparing to share their stories with you. My intention for you as you read through these stories is for them to bring you hope, joy and inspiration to seek out opportunities to find and live your purpose with passion, connect with others, know that you will alway find a solution, no matter how difficult a challenge feels at the time, sometimes it takes courage to be a little vulnerable... there are so many people willing to help you, we sometimes need a little reminder to be brave and just ask!

The proceeds from the sale of this book will be used to support women under 25 in the Edinburgh, Fife and East Lothian area of Scotland. Business Women Connections Edinburgh Futures Group is committed to nurturing the next generation of women leaders and entrepreneurs, offering a safe platform for 16-25-year-olds to network and grow within a community that shares their values and understands the unique challenges they face.

- Find out more about the Business Women Connections Edinburgh Futures Group at: https://www.bwcedinburgh.co.uk/bwc-futures

1

LEADING WITH LOVE

UNSTUCK AND UNSTOPPABLE!

ALVINA MENZIES

"The present moment is filled with joy and happiness. If you are attentive, you will see it."

— *THICH NHAT HANH*

Rewind... 31st March 2021

All I could see was a barefoot child running along the beach, paddling in the water, jumping the waves, joyful and free, released from all responsibility... the innocence, the human experience. In that moment I gave away all the heart strength that I could, to help free his soul, as happy as the child on the sun-drenched beach, to allow him to pass over—this was my very first experience of channelling Reiki healing energy to someone else. Six years after his cancer diagnosis, this was the moment in time that my husband's human experience would end.

Release and Restore

"I'm on my way from misery to happiness..." These are lyrics from one of his favourite songs that played in the background in the moment of his passing. He also used to say 'It is, what it is"... and told us this all the time. We managed a difficult chapter of our lives with a positive attitude, focusing our energies on fundraising to support families and children affected by cancer. Words and heartfelt actions that would continue to comfort and guide us forward as a family.

What now? Little did I know I had given away all of my inner power and energy to help ease his transition—this was only going to come to light for me in the months that lay ahead, through the healing and growth that awaited me; it meant that I would have to learn to surrender and trust the process. But did I know how at the time? No, I definitely didn't but my instincts were strong and my priority was to survive each day and focus on creating a future of joy and happiness for myself and my family, no matter what.

Our inner instincts that respond to stress and fear, fight, take flight or freeze were soon kicking in. I bought our neighbour's blue and white camper van that I'd admired for years and named her Skye. Skye took me on a literal journey of adventure and self awareness, even finding myself on the island of Skye where I experienced profound moments of what I know now were elements of my spiritual, or what I fondly call my heart, awakening. From peering over the top of 'Old Man of Storr' and connecting with my heart, right there in the drizzling rain to finding myself staying at the same campsite on what would have been our 21st wedding anniversary, no planning, just trusting the flow of life. I had forgotten that we had visited together many years before, because we had turned up there by motorbike in the pitch dark in the pouring rain, but that's where I needed to be in that moment and trusted that I had been guided to be there.

Becoming a practitioner (and later training as a trainer) of Emotional CPR & energy healing back in 2019 allowed me to embody these techniques to reconnect with my heart and maintain a positive flow of my inner energy, quickly removing blockages at their root cause through a rapid energy healing technique called Silent Counselling. The creation of my own unique healing combination 'Release & Restore' where I gently release stuck energy 'bubbles' that gather through our conscious thoughts and layers, sometimes presenting as physical dis-ease and restoring this through channelling Reiki healing energy, has been transformative in both my own life and for my clients.

Connecting with people in the heart of my community had also been a huge part of my healing and entrepreneurial journey after leaving the corporate world burnt out, and the Instagram following of 'Adventures of Skye' provided me with a conscious platform to connect, write and share my grief journey throughout that time, in the hope that it would resonate with others and inspire them to focus on their purpose through difficult times, to navigate and live a full life doing whatever they loved most.

Post Traumatic Growth In the Heart of the Community

Standing basking in the warmth of the autumn sun blazing through the floor-to-ceiling alcove window of an old townhouse living room, looking out over the expansive garden that had been the solace of the banker who had lived there many years ago. Looking out over a thriving allotment now filled with colourful flowers and vegetables, watching the gardener who had nurtured this for over twenty years, happy and so very proud of his creation and space.

That's when I felt it... something in my gut, something in my heart, a feeling so strong, something urging me to surrender and trust. In that very moment, an idea was born, to create a beautiful space full of joy and happiness that would bring small business owners and our local community together.

It had only been six months since my husband had passed away, I found myself taking on what the logical brain and the external world —a ridiculously huge risk, but something inside me knew I had to do it, but I didn't even know what 'it' was!

What came next were many gatherings of amazing people who rented office spaces and hosted classes and workshops that would not only serve our community but support me personally to release trauma emotions and build my energy back up, increasing my self awareness and embracing a spiritual healing and awakening journey. Reiki, sound baths, and connecting with others through community and networking events all helped this process, and I was also grateful to participate in a spiritual coaching programme to reconnect with and embrace my feminine energy, to help nurture and restore that part of me.

Once again, I found myself embodying the steps in my coaching programme I had created when leaving the corporate world back in 2018—The SPRING Solution 6 Steps to SUCCESS. By slowing down, consciously, energetically... but this time around I had trained and added powerful subconscious healing techniques to this programme to remove and recode stagnant limiting beliefs and allow reconnection with the heart of my inner child. One example of this was releasing a core fear of not being good enough, sound familiar? This was related to negative emotions passed on to my subconscious in the womb at six months, so absolutely outwith my control, looking back I could see how this had held me back from having the confidence to be my true self, for many years as I followed the conditioned path, meeting the expectations of others, a people pleaser.

Back in 2018, the first time I went through the first exercise I always share at the beginning of my coaching programme 'This is Me', the two things that stood out, what I loved most, was helping people and having a social impact. Looking back I have most definitely achieved this through all of the entrepreneurial activities, fundraising hikes and co-creating a Wellbeing Project, using the healing and relaxation skills of our small business community from within my business hub at 58 Bonnygate in our family hometown in Cupar, Fife.

As I began to take the time to connect more with my inner self, to my heart and to the universe and spirit guides, during meditation I received a very clear message: my purpose is to 'Lead communities of wise successful women.' I felt that I was already doing this but kept it in the back of my mind, reminding myself of this regularly when I reflected and refocused my intentions and aspirations, both personally and professionally.

Stuck under a huge boulder, unable to move a muscle...

That's how I would describe the weight of responsibility I began to feel for the business hub and the people who were relying on using the space to run their businesses. The first winter brought the reality of extortionate electricity bills, together with water and business rates —these systems almost broke me. In my heart though, I had determination and would remain a voice for small businesses, fighting for fairness and opportunities for their growth.

So many questions were spinning around in my head—why did I do this, who did I think I was... I didn't have all the answers, I couldn't possibly do this. What would my husband have said? I reached out to those around me who were more than happy to listen and helped to suggest ways forward, providing solutions ... you don't know what you don't know, but you can definitely learn as you go. It's good to remember that all challenging experiences provide us with lessons in life, love and in business.

I believed in the vision, after all it came from deep within my heart and to this day I continue to navigate to achieve fair outcomes, enabling small business owners and providing them with affordable space to connect, be inspired and thrive together building and growing their businesses. Interestingly, this challenge presented me with yet another unexpected opportunity to heal the subconscious fears that were holding me stuck under that boulder. I don't need to share the details, but what I should share is that this process was life changing for both my mindset and my ability to trust in myself fully and continue to follow my passion.

Stuck In The 'Waiting Room'

2023 was a year of investment in my own personal development, trusting myself that the next chapter was being guided, significant growth was waiting for me... but I needed to learn to be patient and not get frustrated, which I learned is a trait of my human design as a 'Generator'—a creator. As I combined this method with my 'Release & Restore' technique I discovered so much more about myself and how I could balance and activate my creative energy for the best successful outcomes... but I had to remain patient!!! I share with my mentoring and coaching clients about being comfortable working in the 'grey'—becoming comfortable not knowing the outcomes in the present moment and surrendering to whatever will be ahead is meant for you. Easier said than done sometimes though, right?

Always keen to learn, and it seems a serial creator by this stage, I set up another business, property-related this time, with the intention of creating opportunities and generational wealth for my family for the future. This seed was planted as a new generation and renewed hope for our family arrived in October 2023 when I became a granny for the first time, to the most beautiful little boy, reminding us of the innocence, joy and opportunity life holds for us, expansive and without limitations.

December 2023, that's when I felt it again... something in my gut, something in my heart, a feeling so strong, something urging me to surrender and trust. An opportunity had been shared with me, to lead a network and become a voice for women on a much larger scale than I had already in my local community, to help make a positive difference in the world of business and for generations to come.

Like the '58' situation, I knew in my heart this was something I was deeply passionate about, mindful of the 'Boulder phase' lessons though, this time I took a little more time to diligently comb through contracts, the risks, the opportunities, the challenges that any business owner might experience, but the feeling was so strong—I was being called to lead from the heart once again.

Getting Ready To Gallop

Investing in myself, my knowledge and sharing that wisdom took a new turn in January 2024 when I undertook Property Investor training, my intention to understand more about the wealth opportunities this can bring when done right. It would also create opportunities to learn through experience, pass on this knowledge and create opportunities for my clients, for my family and for my future.

I've also always dreamt of becoming an author, sharing wisdom and thoughts with the world. I signed up to write a chapter in a collaborative book called 'Rise of the Female Entrepreneur' for

International Women's Day in March '24. Recognising that I was a 'serial entrepreneur' I was ready to share my story and during this process my passion for writing was growing.

By April I had officially become the owner of the franchise business, Business Women Connections Edinburgh, Fife & East Lothian, a membership and business growth network for women. This experience can only be described as a baptism of fire... typically my style it seems. With only five weeks to organise and host the Annual Awards event for 120 women. Nominations came in across eight categories, with many inspirational achievements and experiences I couldn't wait to share and celebrate.

Hosting this event in May '24 allowed me to step into a space of significant growth, and although there had been a build-up of pressure to deliver one of the best events of the year in the Edinburgh business community. With pure joy and happiness in my heart, I welcomed every single person into the room with a heartfelt hug and stood up on that stage without a second thought, thankful to have been blessed with the opportunity for all of these women to connect and celebrate their successes together.

But... July brought another blow... both mentally and physically, I was forced to slow down again. I found myself walking along my favourite beach in St Andrews, my childhood home town. I watched and felt the ground shudder as horses passed me by. Another message, standing in the energy of the horses, trusting this moment —'Get ready to gallop forward, you have three months to change your life.' In that moment, I made a few conscious decisions that would do just that. Sell my husband's work van, get a new car for my daughter to learn to drive, sell our family home, move on and create freedom for all of my family.

There it was AGAIN... something in my gut, something in my heart, a feeling so strong, something urging me to surrender and trust. A stampede of decisions this time though... in August, leaning into my property knowledge, I bought a 'beach house' holiday lodge in Crail in the East Neuk of Fife. Making decisions based on what my heart was guiding me to do, we also put down a deposit on a new build. In September my son headed off to Australia; I encouraged him to take the opportunity while he could and in October I agreed to an off-market sale of our home which had been the heart of our family for eighteen years.

These transformational decisions and changes also ignited a renewed passion to write, but I wanted to do it by bringing together women from all over the world to tell their stories 'From The Heart'.

I felt that there was something missing from the writing process I had gone through myself back in March and knew I could provide a more meaningful experience, wraparound support, holding space for the healing and growth opportunities that sharing your story with the world can bring to the surface, an opportunity to banish any limiting beliefs and feelings of being stuck, boosting clarity and confidence to lead the way in the world.

I know that my purpose is to use my passion and energy, like the sun, to extend this globally and shine hope and have a positive impact on as many women in leadership and business as possible. What I love most is sharing all that I have learned in my fifty-one years as a human... a leader, a teacher, a guide. This is what brings me the most joy.

Recently, my mindset changed to see my businesses as vehicles—frameworks that I had been guided to create over the six years that are there to help me to deliver this purpose and passion with ease and flow.

We can never be 'healed' completely; we are complex beings, but if we can learn and embody simple ways of slowing down in the present moment, to truly connect with our hearts, recognising when we are stuck, when we are being restricted by conditioned thoughts or experiences, recognising what we can control and cannot, to pause and recognise the joy and happiness in the present moment, it can free your heart, your mind and your soul.

Refocus and New Beginnings

"I love to create JOY and I do this by creating experiential, impactful and community based events and services to connect, inspire so we can thrive together."

SLOW: Stop, Listen, Observe and Welcome—self explanatory words even at a high level. The first module of my coaching programme has served me well over the last six years, and I know now that the anchor statement above is what SUCCESS feels like for me right now.

Six months on from making the decision on that beach walk, to sell our family home of eighteen years, I'm now writing this chapter surrounded by my life in boxes at my mum's house. Exactly four years from the day where I began this chapter, on 31st March 2025, our new home should be ready for us to move into.

A golden thread, connecting and inspiring women across the world to lead from their hearts... that is my vision. Through business mentoring, coaching programmes, healing and building and leading communities through 58 Bonnygate and BWC Edinburgh—the ripple effect is real and my passion to help women get unstuck, find their purpose and live their passion, and thrive every single day for the rest of their lives is stronger than ever.

You will have many choices to make today; we don't know what lies ahead of us but what we do know is that if we connect and always choose to lead from the heart, you will go to sleep every night satisfied that you have done your very best, and that is more than good enough.

My passion is to spread joy across the world, to help you lead from the heart. I love to empower my clients to allow their inner purpose and passion to light the way forward to create their own success.

Please always remember ... You are never alone. There's always a solution. Have the courage to connect, share your challenges, stay aligned to your purpose and passion, lead with love, you will get unstuck, it will all work out, every step is as it is meant to be.

YOU ARE UNSTOPPABLE!

> **"The present moment is filled with joy and happiness. If you are attentive, you will see it."**
>
> — *THICH NHAT HANH*

ABOUT THE AUTHOR

Alvina Menzies radiates warmth, compassion and an inspiring spirit. Her approach to leadership is rooted in a deep understanding of the power of connection and nurturing relationships. By championing women to lead from their hearts, Alvina taps into a beautiful essence that encourages vulnerability, authenticity, and mutual support. Her work in business mentoring and healing coaching is not just about professional success; it's about fostering a sense of community and empowerment among women across the world. Alvina's commitment to creating impactful experiences and events reflects her belief in the transformative power of shared joy and collaboration. This is expressed through her ability to uplift others, helping them break free from limitations and embrace their true potential.

Living near St Andrews in Scotland with her family, Alvina draws inspiration from nature's beauty, which further enhances her connection to the world around her. Her love for travel and exploration reflects her adventurous spirit, always open to new possibilities, embodying the essence of intuition and creativity. Alvina is not just a business leader; she is a beacon of inspiration and a catalyst for change, inviting others to join her on a journey of self-discovery, empowerment, and collective growth.

- https://linktr.ee/alvinamenzies

2

FINDING MY FOOTING

A JOURNEY OF RESILIENCE AND SELF-DISCOVERY

BHARTI RAJPUT

"Behind every brave face is a heart that has carried the weight of countless stories."

For James, who has my heart

You are the rhythm in my words, the fire in my pages, the ink in my veins.

This chapter, like my heart, belongs to you—forever.

I still remember how my mother's hands trembled as she adjusted my necklace on that crisp February morning in 2018. We were inside the taxi en route to the grand halls of Buckingham Palace, the weight of my MBE honour hanging between us like something sacred. My father sat in the front seat, clad in the suit he had tailored especially for the occasion, pride glistening in his typically reserved eyes as he recounted stories of his struggles to this day and how proud he was to accompany his daughter to Buckingham Palace for an award bestowed by the Queen herself. The fact that he never had the opportunity to complete his secondary education mattered little today; in a culture where the education of women and daughters is often given second priority, it was indeed a day of success where my parent's commitment to their daughter's education had triumphed!

I swallowed hard, trying to steady my breathing. The thick red carpet beneath my feet, the chandeliers casting golden hues over the polished wood—it was a scene I had only ever imagined in childhood fairytales. I quieted that voice of imposter syndrome that had haunted me many a time and kept repeating in my head the nursery rhyme...

"Pussycat, pussycat, where have you been?"

"I've been to London to look at the Queen."

And now, here I was. Not a little girl with wide-eyed wonder but a woman who had built something from the ground up. A clinic, a business, a potential *legacy*.

For a moment, I allowed myself to feel it—all the sacrifices, all the late nights, the exhaustion, the risks. The endless battles to keep my business afloat, to prove to myself and the world that I was more than just an ambitious immigrant's daughter. This moment wasn't just for me. It was for my parents, who had left behind everything they knew so their children could have choices. It was for my younger self, who had sat in dimly lit rooms, studying late into the night while her peers were partying under streetlights. It was for every patient I had ever helped take a pain-free step forward.

The medal in my hand felt incredible, so solid, so real.

I exhaled slowly as I shook the hand of the now King of the United Kingdom, who not only congratulated me but addressed me as the "*magic foot lady of Dundee!*" whilst presenting the medal to me.

I was on top of the world, and when a limousine my mother had arranged to pick us up after the ceremony arrived, it felt like the icing on the cake!

"*I don't know if I'll ever see you married. You're so picky about men! I thought we could take a ride in a limo around London today, as I might not get another chance,*" she said in her Indian motherly tone.

I laughed it off. "*Someday, someday, maa, I'll meet my prince charming...just you wait.*"

That day, it felt as though the universe was genuinely listening. Our little family, cruising the streets of London in a limo with a bottle of red Shloer to mark the occasion, felt like the best celebration, and I still remember it as my happiest day so far!

Months later, life gifted me something unexpected.

James walked into my life quietly, without the usual grand romantic gestures. No lightning bolts, no overwhelming intensity—just steady, grounding presence. His love wasn't a storm; it was the warmth of the sun after a long, cold winter. Seven months later, we held the keys to our dream cottage in Scotland—in a small commuting village we had both envisioned without ever realising it.

The stone walls felt permanent, as if they had witnessed lifetimes before ours and would witness many after. The land stretched out in rolling hills, and the air was crisp and full of promise.

For the first time in years, I felt settled. *Whole.*

New Year's Eve arrived, and as I watched our parents celebrate Hogmanay with us, my mind flickered back to another New Year's Eve—standing in London as fireworks burst across the sky, feeling the undeniable pull of a new decade.

The turn of 2000 felt the same: a *new beginning*, a fresh slate. Even Oprah, whom I have admired for as long as I can remember, spoke of 2020 as the year of vision and purpose.

And so, I made plans—*big* ones.

I booked a ticket to her *Your Life in Focus* tour in New York.

If there was anyone who could inspire me to reach even greater heights, it was Oprah.

New York felt electric. The first two days were everything I had imagined: meeting like-minded people, absorbing wisdom, and feeling a renewed sense of clarity.

And then, on the third day, something shifted.

It started as a heaviness in my limbs, an inexplicable sluggishness. I reassured myself it was exhaustion or perhaps the small indulgence in too many bagels, too much pizza, and too much pastrami. Yet, deep down, I knew better.

Standing outside the Rockefeller Centre, my last stop before flying home, I felt something foreign settle inside me. I should have been excited. *I was always excited*—always the one with a never-ending list of places to see and things to do. But that night, I *Facetimed* my mother standing outside the Rockefeller Centre and said something I had never said.

"I just can't be bothered."

The words felt foreign on my tongue.

Dragging myself to the observation deck, I forced myself to take in the view. The lights of Manhattan spread out like veins beneath me, but I felt nothing.

The next morning, I boarded my flight home with a fever burning beneath my skin.

By the time I landed, I was drowning in sickness.

The coughing started immediately. Violent, relentless, as if my lungs were trying to escape my body. My head ached. My muscles screamed. My body *did not feel like my own.*

At that time, COVID was still merely a whisper around the globe, restricted to headlines concerning China. But as I lay in bed, too weak to move, I knew.

I called my GP.

"Just a viral flu," he said.

But it wasn't.

It *wasn't.*

Two weeks later, my fever broke, but my body was different. The fatigue clung to me like a second skin. My mind was wrapped in fog so thick I struggled to remember simple things.

Still, I forced myself back to work.

Because *that's what I did.* I persevered. I had never taken time off before—never permitted myself the luxury of pausing.

And then, the whispers of COVID turned into screams.

One Friday evening, as I sat by the fire, sipping a hot toddy, still nursing the remnants of this 'flu', I read the news: our local health centre had reported the first case of the virus.

My stomach knotted. I rang a colleague.

"What shall we do if it actually reaches us?" I enquired.

He let out a humourless laugh.

"Bharti, it's already here."

The weekend passed quickly. Patients started cancelling appointments, and fear crept into the clinic like an uninvited guest.

On March 23rd 2020, the government announced a national lockdown.

On March 24th, we treated our last patients.

On March 25th, a neighbour called. Someone had tried to break into the clinic overnight!

I frantically organised a window-boarding company, fearful that my business would be vandalised during this vacant period. There were reports of nearby local businesses having their windows smashed for the sake of some coins in a charity tin at the till! I now stood outside my boarded-up business, staring at the plywood sealing away my life's work.

I had built this with my own hands.

And now, it felt like my thriving business had been boxed into a coffin, *it was dead*!

I sank onto the steps, my body folding in on itself, and sobbed.

Because for the first time in my life, I didn't know what came next.

The first week after I locked my clinic doors, I moved through life in a daze. My body still felt foreign, and my mind was disconnected from everything I had created. I wandered through our cottage, my fingers trailing over bookshelves, counters, and window panes—searching for *something*.

But what?

Who was I without my clinic? Without my patients?

Without my *purpose*?

I had poured everything into my business—every late night, every ounce of energy, every part of myself. And now, with a world in lockdown, my life had been paused, as if someone had pressed a cruel, invisible button.

And then, guilt.

Because I wasn't *just* mourning the loss of work; I was mourning the loss of identity.

Other people had lost loved ones. Others were suffering in hospitals, alone, their lungs failing them. And here I was, *grieving a business*.

That self-recrimination sat heavy in my chest.

I needed to *do* something.

So, I drove to the clinic to check on the building and gathered supplies. I filled the boot of my car with nail files, padding, and ointments—small things that could help my patients from a distance. I wrote handwritten notes of encouragement and sealed them in envelopes.

Maybe I couldn't heal their feet in person, but I could still *help*.

And yet, every night, as I lay in bed next to James, staring at the ceiling, a different thought gnawed at me.

Who would I be if I wasn't *Dr B, the podiatrist*?

In the next few weeks, I threw myself into organisation mode, which I could control, of course. I neatly organised all my digital and paper files, making myself feel useful.

Then, a mirror appeared that I didn't wish to confront, or was it a mirror that wanted to confront me?

I discovered it concealed beneath a pile of forgotten papers in my home filing cabinet.

The *Wheel of Life* worksheet.

At the start of each year, I always gave this to my team, encouraging them to reflect on their balance—work, relationships, health, finances, and personal growth.

Yet I had not filled one out myself in a very long time.

Until that night.

I picked up a pen, my fingers trembling slightly, and began marking my scores.

Career? 9/10. Romance? 8/10.

Everything else?

Below a 3.

A sinking sensation settled in my stomach.

I had spent my entire life building my business, ensuring my patients walked pain-free and that my team had a vision to follow. I had spent so much time taking care of *everyone else that* I hadn't even realised how little of my own life I had nurtured.

I didn't have hobbies, a strong circle of friends outside of work, or any*thing* beyond my career.

The realisation hit me like a gut punch.

And yet, even as I sat there, staring at those numbers, something in me stirred. A small, quiet voice.

"You can change this."

As weeks passed, I forced myself to lean into *stillness*.

I journaled every day, expressing the emotions I had long suppressed. I wrote about the grief, the anger, and the fear. I detailed how much I hated slowing down and how it made me feel *useless*.

I felt the waves of grief cycle through me. Denial. Anger. Blame. Guilt. Acceptance.

Some days, I believed I was healing. Others, I felt like I was drowning.

But through it all, I kept *moving*.

When the restrictions eased, I adapted. I installed protective screens at the clinic, changed treatment protocols, and triaged urgent cases.

I *pushed through*, just as I always had.

Rebuilding a business as we entered third and second lockdowns was challenging enough, and then ...

The betrayal.

James had been my steady force throughout the chaos. He had stepped into the business, helping in ways I hadn't even realised I needed.

And then, she happened.

One of my staff members—someone I had trusted. Someone who, behind closed doors, sexually assaulted him!

People often talk about sexual misconduct by men —like in the #MeToo movement. But what about when the perpetrator is a woman?

But it happened. And when I found out, I felt something inside me *snap*.

I had built my team on trust and *care*. I had fostered a family, not merely a workplace. And now, one of my own had shattered that.

As a small team, it was considered best to conduct a fair investigation without my involvement, and a member of the leadership team was deemed the most suitable person to support us in ensuring that we acted fairly, as any reputable business would.

There are always two sides to every story, and all I wanted was for both to be heard to truly understand what prompted such an act that no one should ever have to endure, particularly in a workplace.

A fair investigation was not carried out internally, and James became the subject of further indirect discrimination. The team was divided. It became *them versus us*.

I had spent *years* building this team. And just like that, it crumbled.

Legal battles drained funds meant for business growth. The independent investigation was long, gruelling, and *soul-destroying*.

The woman was found guilty.

But the damage was done.

The trust was gone. The toxicity had seeped in too deep.

I made the hardest decision of my life.

I dismantled what I had built, brick by brick, until I stood alone in my clinic.

I had always feared losing my business.

I never realised I would have to *break it down myself* just to save it.

But from the rubble, I began again.

I rebuilt—this time with a team that upheld the values of the business, a team I could trust. A team that truly believed in the vision I had worked so hard to create.

Not long after, James's body started betraying him.

It began with his eye—his left eyelid drooping, refusing to stay open.

Optician after optician. Tests upon tests.

The anxiety clawed at my chest as we waited for answers. Was it a stroke? A blood clot? A tumour?

Then, the diagnosis.

Myasthenia gravis.

An autoimmune disease. Chronic.

He lost his peripheral vision. He couldn't drive. The man who had always been strong, who had held *me* up, was now struggling to hold himself together.

James's admission to the hospital for immunotherapy was both a relief and held a heavy shadow of uncertainty. The stark white walls, the hushed voices of nurses moving between patients and the rhythmic beeping of monitors—it all felt eerily clinical. Yet here we were, hoping this treatment would offer him some stability.

I sat by his bedside, watching as the IV slowly delivered the antibodies his body desperately needed to combat the myasthenia gravis that had so cruelly sapped his strength. He gave my hand a gentle squeeze, his lips curling into a reassuring smile, but I could see the exhaustion in his eyes, the weight of uncertainty pressing down on us both. There were no guarantees—no certainty that this would work, no promise that his vision would return, and no clear understanding of what the future held.

Yet, as I sat there, gripping his fingers tightly, I felt a deep, humbling gratitude—for the NHS, for the doctors who had spent years studying this rare condition, for the nurses who moved through the ward with quiet kindness, and for the privilege of accessing care when so many in the world went without.

When the infusions were done, another battle began—long-term steroids. A necessary evil. They held the disease at bay, but they came at a price—weight gain, muscle cramps and sleepless nights, a body that no longer felt like his own.

Every morning, as he reached for the blister pack of tablets, I saw the silent war he was waging—not just against his condition but against the sheer emotional toll of it all. And yet, he never once complained. Instead, we faced it together, side by side, adapting to this new version of life with cautious optimism, grateful for every day, for every small improvement, for every fleeting moment of normality.

And I?

I was already *running on empty*.

But life wasn't done with me yet.

One morning, I noticed a white patch on my left eyelid. I ignored it. A week later, another appeared, and then another.

Vitiligo.

An autoimmune disease with no cure!

I was referred to a dermatologist who told me about the low success rate of any steroid creams or UV light therapy and that I just had to go into acceptance!

Go into acceptance?

My body was attacking itself, erasing my colour in patches.

I spent hours researching the Internet, something I would continue to do at times. As I write this chapter, there remains no definitive cure for vitiligo.

Throughout my life, I have worn my skin with pride, even when the Indian aunties labelled me as *dark!*, colourism in my community, from my own people at best! Now, when I look into the mirror, occasionally, I feel like I am *fading,* but then I remind myself of the other parts of my body that function well and immerse myself in gratitude.

By Christmas 2022, I had nothing left to give.

Burnt out. Mentally wrecked. Physically deteriorating.

Then, a fever of 39.5°C. James begged me to go to the hospital. I refused at the start as our first proper holiday was booked only four days later, and I didn't want to ruin it.

On Christmas Eve, I felt considerably worse and admitted that I needed to go to the hospital. I was placed on oxygen, and the only thing I remember is seeing a constant bright light as if the angels were enveloping me in their protective, healing glow.

Four days later, we boarded a flight to Goa. I was still unwell but determined to travel. James was quite worried but maintained a brave face. I was also concerned for him, given the amount of steroids he was taking. Although we had received clearance from his neurologist, it was a worrying time, and I was putting on a brave face, too.

We both discovered *stillness* in Goa. We nourished our bodies with the most exquisite Ayurvedic vegetarian food, engaged in physical movement, and learned Yoga poses together. I could not, and still cannot, touch my toes as well as he can, but James, my flexible 6-foot-3 Viking, glided through the yoga poses with such grace.

My feet sank into the warm sand, and the sound of the waves crashing rhythmically against the shore became my sanctuary, a natural metronome for my breath as I tried to find some sense of peace after the storm of the last few years. James and I had arrived here exhausted—physically, mentally, and emotionally—each carrying invisible scars from the relentless battles we had faced. We learned to listen to the waves. To breathe deeply. To allow ourselves to rest without guilt.

I had spent years ignoring the messages my body was trying to send me. The fatigue, the brain fog, the aching joints, the vitiligo that had begun spreading across my skin—it was all stress, but I hadn't truly understood its depth. I had always been someone who pushed through, who carried the weight of everything and everyone without a second thought for myself. But for the first time in years, I slowed down. I listened. As I sat there, watching the horizon stretch endlessly in front of me, I began researching how chronic stress affects the body—not just in the abstract sense, but biologically, physiologically, and measurably.

That's when I found it.

Heart Rate Variability.

A simple yet profound concept: HRV is the variation in time between each heartbeat—a reflection of how effectively the autonomic nervous system is functioning. Unlike a standard heart rate measurement, which simply indicates how fast your heart is beating, HRV offers insight into the balance between the sympathetic (fight-or-flight) and parasympathetic (rest-and-digest) nervous systems. A high HRV typically signifies a more adaptable and resilient nervous system, whereas a low HRV may indicate chronic stress, fatigue, or even underlying health issues.

I read study after study, each reaffirming something I had always known intuitively but had never been able to quantify—stress wasn't just an emotional state; it was something we could measure and influence.

I learned that HRV isn't static—it can be improved. And one of the most powerful ways to do that?

Targeted breathwork.

Deep, controlled breathing activates the vagus nerve, the main component of the parasympathetic nervous system. This nerve, in turn, increases HRV and signals to the body that it is safe. The more I explored, the more I realised that breath is one of the most underutilised tools for regulating our nervous system, shifting from stress to calm, from chaos to clarity.

It wasn't about complicated techniques. It was about slowing down, breathing with intention, syncing my breath with my heartbeat in a way that told my body, *You are safe. You can rest now.*

I decided to put it to the test.

I ordered a heart rate variability monitor—one that could track my levels in real-time. The first reading?

Shockingly low.

My body had been stuck in fight-or-flight for so long that I barely knew what true relaxation felt like. No wonder I had developed an autoimmune condition. No wonder my brain felt like it was wading through fog every single day.

I started with coherent breathing—slow, rhythmic breaths, six per minute, in through the nose for five seconds, out through the mouth for five seconds. I practised it every morning before I checked my phone before I let the noise of the world in.

And slowly, things changed.

My sleep improved. The tinnitus that had plagued me for months began to fade. My focus sharpened. The weight I had been carrying in my chest—the one I had barely acknowledged—began to lift.

For the first time in years, I felt like I was healing.

When I returned to my clinic, something had shifted—not just within me, but within my patients.

I had always been a podiatrist, someone who focused on the mechanics of walking, movement, and pain relief.

But suddenly, I started to notice something else. The tension in my patients' bodies. The anxious way they sat in the chair, their breath shallow, their shoulders tight, their words tinged with uncertainty.

It wasn't just foot pain that had brought them in.

It was anxiety.

It was fear of the future, of what their life would look like in this new world after COVID.

It was the uncertainty of their health, the creeping awareness that their bodies were holding onto more stress than they realised.

It was a different kind of pain—not just physical, but emotional and psychological, deeply ingrained in their nervous systems.

The pandemic had changed the way people lived, worked, and socialised. It had left scars, even on those who had never caught the virus. And I could see it, sitting in front of me, etched into the very fabric of my patients' lives.

I knew I had to do something different.

It was no longer enough to just treat the feet. I needed to help the person behind them.

I became a HeartMath coach, diving deep into the science of HRV training, stress management, and emotional resilience. I studied how coherent breathing, biofeedback, and self-regulation techniques could improve not just physical health but mental clarity, emotional well-being, and overall vitality. I also qualified as a certified wellness coach, expanding my focus beyond biomechanics to encompass stress, sleep, anxiety, and nervous system regulation.

I changed the way I practised.

Now, when patients come to me, we don't just talk about their feet—we talk about how they feel, how they sleep, and how they breathe. We track HRV in the clinic and introduce small, achievable changes that help them regain control of their nervous systems.

Because foot pain is rarely *just* about the feet.

Stress affects posture, gait, circulation, and inflammation. It influences how we move, how we heal, and how we live.

By addressing the whole person, I realised I could help my patients not just walk better but live better.

I am still on this journey.

I am still learning, still healing, and still uncovering new layers of myself.

But I know this much—I am not just a podiatrist. I am not just a business owner. I am not just someone who fixes foot pain.

I am someone who sees the whole person.

I understand what it means to carry stress in the body, to hold grief in the bones, to push through burnout until the body forces you to stop.

I am a podiatrist, a wellness coach, a HeartMath coach, and a guide for those who are searching for more than just relief from foot pain—they are searching for balance, healing, for a way to feel whole again.

Because we don't just walk through life on autopilot; we carry our experiences, our fears, and our anxieties in every step we take.

And now, I help people find their footing—not just on the outside but within themselves.

One breath at a time.

Today, my life is different.

I have a new team. A new purpose. It's like my version 2.0.

I paint, I write, we cook from scratch, and we enjoy the garden. I'm also an aspiring beekeeper and dream of getting my private pilot's license someday.

"Go, Girl! Fly! High into the Sky" is my mantra!

As I write this, my face is now 80% depigmented, and the white patches continue to spread across my body. I am learning to camouflage with makeup on the days I feel the need to enhance my appearance to show up, and I love myself more than ever before. However, some days are harder than others; I find encouragement in the media and advertisements that promote inclusivity for people with vitiligo, making it increasingly more normal. James never fails to kiss me each morning when I wake up and tell me how beautiful I am, reminding me daily that true beauty is a light that comes from within the heart. It doesn't matter whether I am brown or white; in my heart, I'm still Bharti, a loving, caring, fun, and bubbly girl who wants to live her best life while helping others.

Every Sunday, James and I turn off our phones, step into nature, and *just be*.

Because life isn't about running on empty.

It isn't about pushing through pain, about burning out in the name of ambition.

It's about balance. About knowing when to fight and when to rest.

"Life is Goldilocks porridge," I say now. *"Not too hot. Not too cold. Just right."*

Because behind every brave face is a heart that has carried the weight of countless stories.

And now, I carry mine *differently*.

ABOUT THE AUTHOR

Dr. Bharti Rajput MBE, PhD (also known as Dr B), is a multi-award-winning podiatrist, honoured by the Queen with an MBE for her services to Podiatry and the economy of Dundee in the Queen's Birthday Honours List in 2017.

After qualifying as a Podiatrist at The London Foot Hospital, she started her career in the NHS and private practice. Then she pursued an academic career at the University of Dundee, where she also completed her PhD in Biomechanics and Human Movement Analysis before establishing her flagship clinic in 2011 Dundee. There, alongside her team, she built a thriving specialist foot care practice recognised as Scotland's most enterprising business in 2016.

Today Dr. Bharti's work is focused not only on improving the physical health of her patients but also on supporting their emotional well-being. When she's not helping others step into happiness, she enjoys expressing her creative talents with writing and painting, travelling, exploring nature, and experimenting with spice-infused recipes in her kitchen.

- https://solebodysoul.com/

3

THE POWER OF JOYFUL PRODUCTIVITY

A LIFE-CHANGING JOURNEY

CLAUDIA ROMERO

To my boys (husband included!), my family in Chile, my besties, my friends, and everyone who has crossed my path—I'm forever grateful. You've all shaped me into the person I am today. - Claudia

As a child, life felt like a puzzle with too many missing pieces, and for the first few years, I didn't even realise there was a bigger picture. I was too young to understand what it was, but I was already learning how to face challenges that felt far larger than me—moments when life doesn't just hand you lemons but throws them in your path.

In 1970s Chile, survival overshadowed dreams. "Life isn't like that," my family would say, and while I didn't fully understand, I felt the weight of their words pressing into the air around us—an air you didn't just breathe but carried. At that time, I didn't fully understand the fear, but felt it. It wasn't the kind of fear from monsters under the bed, but the kind that lingered in my mum's glance at the door mid-conversation or in my dad's shoulders tensing whenever he heard the news on the radio.

The coup d'état of 1973 felt like distant thunder—too far for me to understand as I was just a baby. But for my family, everything changed. I grew up feeling their fear and the aftermath of life around me. The country changed overnight—you could feel the tension and sadness. Neighbours who once shared laughs and empanadas now avoided eye contact. Some just disappeared, leaving behind only faint traces of their lives, while the rest stayed silent—not because they wanted to, but because they had to. We were living in a country where even basic rights were stripped away for many, and the air was filled with pressure and fear. Life as many knew it was gone. The streets grew quiet, with abandoned bicycles and forgotten toys serving as silent witnesses to the change. But for me, that was the starting point, this would become my normal, and those small moments taught me to be cautious long before I even knew what that meant.

My parents did everything they could inside our house to prevent the storm outside from tearing us apart. My dad, a former Navy officer, was disciplined and spoke with authority when needed, yet beneath that tough exterior, he was kind and shone through in his care for us. He balanced hard work with fun, teaching us how to ride bikes and swim, always with patience and hugs. My mother, a university professor, embed in us a curiosity and love for learning. She taught us the value of responsibility but also knew when we needed a shoulder to cry on. From them, I learned the value of balance—between duty, joy, and care.

Many years passed living in a place where you were constantly walking over eggshells, knowing that the wrong words could bring everything down. At home, we spoke freely—but even then, with caution.

Outside, we became invisible and masters of silence. I remember how my mum's hand would tighten ever so slightly on my shoulder if I said too much in public, a reminder to be careful. The fear wasn't paralyzing, but it was always there, like a shadow you couldn't shake.

I was still an 8-year-old girl who just wanted to be a child, finding joy in small, stolen moments despite the chaos around me. For me, joy was simple: sleeping in, laughing with friends, and avoiding homework. Oh, how I loved my sleep! Even now, it's a running joke. But back then, it wasn't just laziness (okay, maybe a bit!). I knew if I wanted my moments of fun, I had to earn them. So, I powered through homework, chores, and responsibilities like I was racing to the finish line. The faster and better I completed them, the harder it was for anyone to say, "No, you can't go out."

What began as a child's strategy to maximise playtime became something much deeper than time management. I was learning resilience—not the kind that fights every battle, but the kind that chooses its battles wisely and finds joy despite the chaos. I wasn't trying to be productive; I just wanted to maximize the things that mattered to me—fun, friends, and, most of all, sleep.

And yes, I had a lot of fun—not everything was so dark. I had the best friends I could have, and we went out, laughed and daydreamed about the boys we liked. Summers were filled with anecdotes that we still remember even now. It's almost surreal how we balanced so well on that thin line between normalcy and chaos. My bubble was intact, and the ugly reality so many others lived with was outside of my scope.

The fear stayed with me as I got older. I stopped noticing how easily I second-guessed myself, avoided certain topics, and hid my true thoughts. On the outside, my life seemed carefree, but underneath, I had built a shield.

Finding Freedom

The change to democracy in Chile was like the first ray of light after a long, stormy night—a spark of hope that did not wipe the slate clean of the past but promised that maybe someday it would. It was 1989, and Chile faced a critical referendum to either continue with democratic elections or remain under dictatorship. Tension was in the air; you could feel it, you could hear it everywhere—the protests of people demanding change. Inequality weighed on those already suffering, and just getting by felt like a struggle because of the high cost of living.

These struggles affected my family too, although we did manage to keep our heads above the water. Both my parents were working hard; long hours testified to their resilience. Two of my siblings were already working by that time and I was focusing on finishing school. We led simple lives—no luxuries—but we did have a certain stability, something not many could brag of in those days.

All this changed in 1990. The dictatorship fell, democracy returned, and for the first time, I felt the invisible chains loosen. The air was lighter; you could smell freedom—freedom to speak, to question, and to learn the painful truths of the years we'd struggled in silence. But the truth wasn't kind. It showed a world full of pain (which still is felt today), loss, and injustice.

I wasn't a child anymore; I was a teenager, caught between hope and the weight of the past.

My parents were hopeful but measured. "Change is slow," my dad would say, his eyes heavy with years of caution. My mum always believed that education was a way to a stronger and better country. Their words stuck with me, but I was still trying to figure out what they meant to me.

Even so, the fear that had shaped me for 18 years did not just disappear. It had taken root too deep, changing how I thought, spoke, and navigated the world. But for the first time, I could see a future where I could dream without limits.

Going to university was a huge turning point in my studies and for me as a person. This was the very first time I had gotten out of this safe little bubble that my parents and school had created around me. Suddenly, the world became much bigger, louder, and more complicated than I thought. It was the first time I had ever heard stories of people living completely different lives for the past 18 years, people who'd experienced struggles and challenges that I never even thought of. I felt it in my gut—how much I had not known, how much my parents had striven to shield me from. I felt a mix of emotions: anger at how unfair life could be, sadness for what others had gone through, and a new kind of gratitude for all the sacrifices my parents had made to give me a better start.

I realised how much my parents and school shaped the way I thought and acted. It wasn't just their strength to keep going but also their sense of caution. Even as I started finding my own voice and way of seeing the world, their voices were always in the back of my mind, guiding me.

More than anything, growing up back then taught me this: life isn't just getting through the tough times; it's finding meaning and light in the middle of it all. Squeezing every drop out of the lemons that life hands you and making the best of it—not just to survive but to build something stronger in the process.

University was where my safe, quiet bubble finally burst. It was terrifying and freeing all at once, full of stumbles, doubts, and hard lessons learned. But through the chaos—late-night study sessions, endless assignments, and trying to squeeze in a social life—I started discovering who I truly was and who I wanted to be. I wanted to strive, not just to survive, and use the resilience and resourcefulness from my childhood to build something meaningful. Those habits I'd honed as a kid came through: prioritising what mattered most helped me stay on top of my studies, build lifelong friendships, and fiercely protect my sleep—because, honestly, my sanity depended on it!

In my last years at university, I lost my dad—a constant presence who had taught me resilience and responsibility. His passing shook me but also gave me a new perspective: to honour his lessons by focusing on what truly mattered and to make the most of life.

Now, I can see how everything started falling into place during that time. My ability to get things done, keep it all together, and focus on what really mattered wasn't just luck; it was something I'd been working on since I was 8 years old. Friends even joked that I was the "get-it-done girl" because I always juggled everything without stress. What they didn't see was that I wasn't driven by duty but joy. I did it because it gave me the freedom to enjoy life. And to me, that freedom meant everything.

After university, I entered the working world and soon learned that if I wanted to develop my career, mastering English for Business wasn't a bonus; it was a must. Staying in Chile wasn't going to cut it; I needed to immerse myself somewhere that would force me out of my comfort zone. When the opportunity to move to London came up, I said yes. Was I terrified? Absolutely. A new culture, a new country, and a language I'd only practised in classrooms—it was a lot to take on, especially since I'd never even travelled alone before!

Living in London was life-changing. It could not have been more different from the cautious, buttoned-up world I'd known. People spoke their minds without hesitation or fear of consequences. It was almost like stepping into the light after years in the shadows—metaphorically, that is, because the sun wasn't exactly a frequent visitor. I was amazed at the diversity, the bold perspectives, and the refreshing honesty of it all.

While there, I worked and explored Europe, building friendships that have withstood the test of time. Home, however, was calling me, so back to Chile I went, ready to plunge into adulthood headfirst.

I started working at Codelco, a giant in the mining industry and a heavily male-dominated world. Managing budgets, procurement, and contracts, I thrived on turning chaos into order. Every day was a challenge—not just to prove myself as a woman, but as someone who could grasp the industry's complexities. Determined to show I was more than just a "girl who did the math," I used what little free time I had (a miracle, really) to take an Environmental Audit course. My goal? To help my department achieve ISO 14,000 for a sustainable Environmental Management System. I thrived in the whirlwind, never feeling burned out, because I always made time for myself and the things that brought me joy.

After a long time of not having a proper holiday, I took a break and flew back to London to see my friends. I had no idea the trip would change my life forever.

My friends had a party already scheduled on the day I arrived. After the flight, I was barely hanging on, managing just an hour's nap before we were off. They were supposed to meet someone at a Canada Day party at 6 pm, but one friend had her boss's birthday party at lunch. She swore she'd be quick but ended up staying way longer than expected, so we were running late for the Canada Day party. My friend mumbled under her breath, "Stephen is going to kill me. He hates it when I'm late for anything." To lighten the mood, I chuckled and said, "Just blame me. Tell him I made you late—I'll never see him again anyway!"

Fate, it seemed, had other plans. Stephen was charming and funny and, it turned out, unexpectedly captivating. And it further turned out I was to see him again. In fact, 24 years later, we're still together.

The Beginning of a New Stage: Moving to Scotland and the End of a Simple Life

Not long after Stephen and I got married, we had a big decision to make. He received an offer for a job in Scotland. It seemed like a gamble, trading the sun and warmth of Chile for the often unpredictable, rainy skies of Edinburgh. But we told ourselves it was temporary, just a couple of years to see where life would lead us.

The early days in Scotland were anything but easy. That first summer felt non-existent, swallowed by grey skies and damp afternoons. Never in my life had I seen winters so cold and dark, and it tested me to the limit. I missed my family, my friends, the food, and the comfort of life back in Chile. But giving up is not in my nature (I am quite stubborn, to be honest) so I kept going, adapting, and little by little, we started building our life together.

Not long after that, we began our family. The joy of expecting motherhood was met by the heartbreak of going through two miscarriages. They were devastating experiences but they taught us how to be resilient. We eventually welcomed our first son, a ray of light who was followed by his baby brother just 16 months later. The happiness of our growing family was tempered again by a third miscarriage, but two years later, our youngest son was born. That's when our lives took a turn we never could have anticipated.

Our youngest, Christian, was diagnosed with a rare syndrome, and the prognosis was grim. I remember a doctor telling us he would not live through his first year. It felt like the earth had opened up and was swallowing me whole. But Stephen and I wouldn't accept that quietly, and we fought hard—researching relentlessly, questioning every medical decision, advocating tirelessly for Christian's care. We were blessed to have a neuro team that saw us not just as another family but as partners in Christian's journey.

The early years were a whirlwind of hospital stays, sleepless nights, and balancing life with three boys under the age of three and a half—all without family nearby. Stephen's family was in North America, mine in Chile, and support felt distant. Yet, we managed. Family members travelled from time to time to help and one of my sisters, able to work remotely (a rarity pre-COVID), came for extended stays to help with the older boys, while Stephen and I tag-teamed hospital visits. We were a team, and our bond was strengthened by the challenges we faced.

Then came a year that tested us again: while Christian's condition stabilised but still needed stays at the hospital, Santiago, our middle son, suffered a severe accident. Suddenly, we had two boys in the hospital. Then countless appointments for both boys, it was a period marked by exhaustion and worry, yet somehow, we found a way through.

As Christian's needs stabilised, we settled into a new rhythm. It wasn't the life we'd envisioned, but it was ours. Christian required full-time care—he couldn't walk, talk, eat, or move independently—but we adapted.

His life taught us to see the world differently, appreciate little things, and advocate for accessibility and inclusion.

Through it all, we refused to let his condition limit our family experiences, we did what any normal family would do, going on holidays, camping, exploring caves, climbing trees, going to sports events and even having a lifetime experience of riding a speedboat in the Firth of Forth! That taught our other boys to have empathy and resilience.

During these years, I started my first business: a clothing line designed for people with special needs. It was a passion project born out of necessity and run with determination. Balancing business and Christian's care while still raising two energetic boys wasn't easy, but with Stephen's support and the boys' help at home, we made it work.

But again, life decided to throw another curveball. Our eldest, Sebastian, was diagnosed with high-functioning autism and Oppositional Defiant Disorder. That added a whole new layer of complexity to our family routines. With Christian's medical appointments and Sebastian's therapies, our plate was full, to say the least. But no matter what, I just had to prove to my boys that I would never miss a single sports day, school play, or anything family-related even if it killed me—running mostly on little or no sleep. Yes, that is how I learned to run on almost no deep sleep.

Over time, I began to realise that the systems I'd developed to keep our lives afloat weren't just survival tools; they were my superpower. Friends and other mums were amazed at how I managed to stay organised and calm despite everything. That's when the seed of my coaching business was planted. I wanted to help others reclaim their time and take control of their lives.

Years later, I closed my clothing business after a major brand entered the market with a similar product line. It was a devastating moment but a sign that I had to put my energy into coaching and helping clients find their balance and purpose in life.

Things were going well...but then another blow came: the COVID pandemic. We had to learn how to survive all at home. I had to learn how to do all the therapies that Christian was receiving at school and support my boys with their studies while trying to build up a business. We managed and realised that it is possible to juggle and achieve.

When the world started to get normal again, and I had all my illusions about growing my business I was diagnosed with breast cancer. Even as I faced treatment, I continued coaching and caring for Christian. By then, my older boys were old enough to provide invaluable support, for which I'll always be grateful. But just as I began to recover and start rebuilding, the unthinkable happened in October 2023. Our world shattered into a million pieces, and so did my heart—Christian passed away.

His loss was immeasurable. I took time to grieve, process, and heal. Though short, Christian's life left a profound impact. He taught us that strength comes in many forms and that life is never black and white. We celebrate his legacy every day, drawing on the lessons he left us.

Looking back, I see that it was then the seeds of joyful

productivity were planted in those very early years, finding pockets of freedom and joy in a world determined to take them away.

My mission became clear: helping others live with intention, finding priority in what really matters, and finding joy in the midst of adversity. Life is short. Life is uncertain. But it's also damn beautiful. It's not about making lemonade when life gives you lemons; it's about planting the seeds, nurturing them, and then watching something far greater grow.

That is exactly what I help business owners do: simplify, organize, understand, and leverage their time to take back at least eight hours a week for the things that truly matter and scale a successful and sustainable business. Using my S.O.U.L. System, I show them that productivity doesn't mean squeezing in more; it's all about making space for what fuels success and happiness.

If I had to leave you with three productivity truths, they would be:

- Stop glamorising busyness – Productivity is not about doing more; it's about doing what moves the needle.
- Structure brings freedom – The right systems don't box you in; they give you more time to fully live.
- Your time is not refundable, so spend it with intention; no amount of success is worth burnout.

Joyful productivity is not a myth; it's a choice. And when you learn to make time work for you, that's when real freedom starts.

Because at the end of the day, time is the one thing you can never earn back—so spend it like it damn well matters.

ABOUT THE AUTHOR

Claudia Romero is a Time Management and Productivity Consultant who helps business owners feeling overwhelmed, burnout, or stuck in the cycle of trading their life for work. Using her S.O.U.L. system—Simplify, Organise, Understand, and Leverage—she helps them reclaim 8 hours a week, creating space for family, hobbies, and joyful living.

Her expertise comes from thriving in high-pressure corporate roles—where it took three people to replace her—running two businesses, and raising three sons, two with additional needs. The loss of one of her sons profoundly shaped her perspective on balance and what truly matters in life.

Despite life's challenges, Claudia has mastered the art of living productively without feeling overwhelmed. She shares her insights at conferences, inspiring others to embrace joyful productivity. Originally from Chile, Claudia now lives in Scotland with her family and her beloved cat, Edge, who supervises her workdays with a touch of mischief.

- https://claudia-romero.com/

4

THE DANDELION'S JOURNEY

DANIELLE GAFFNEY DU PLOOY

Nature, in its infinite wisdom, provides a mirror to our own journey, helping us navigate life's complexities with greater understanding and grace. Its metaphors offer profound lessons, teaching us about resilience, adaptability, growth, the cyclical nature of existence, and the beauty of impermanence. By observing nature, we gain insights that can guide us through challenges, deepen our self-awareness, and illuminate our connection to the world and the universe.

Take the dandelion, for example: often underestimated, yet so full of hidden secrets. Is it strange to admire the humble dandelion as a metaphor for life, even for leadership? Dandelions hold a significance that transcends their modest appearance, rich with meaning in folklore, mythology, literature, and art. These vibrant yellow flowers, with their delicate puffball seeds, have captured my imagination and my heart. The dandelion's journey, from bright bloom to seed carrier, spreading its essence far and wide, to its persistent reappearance in the most unexpected places, is one of resilience, purpose, and continuous transformation.

In this chapter, I want to share my own journey of growth and transformation, guided by the lessons I've uncovered along the way. Like the dandelion, I've faced challenges, adapted to changing circumstances, and found strength in the most surprising places.

This story is not just about who I was or who I've become but about the ongoing cycles of change, discovery, and renewal that define a life truly lived.

Perspective Shapes Reality

The dandelion challenges us to rethink our perceptions. Where one might see an unwelcome weed, another sees a beacon of joy, its vibrant yellow blossoms a reminder of sunny days and its fluffy seeds, carriers of dreams and wishes. This humble plant teaches us a vital lesson: in life, as with dandelions, our perspective shapes our reality.

Perception and being aware of my viewpoints have been something I've reflected on for years, and to this day, I regularly check in with myself: How am I looking at things? This awareness is something I learned from my mom. When I was younger, in my teens, my family and I went through significant trauma and difficulties. At the time, as I was just transitioning into adulthood, I couldn't fully understand what my parents were facing. It wasn't until years later that I came to appreciate the battles they were quietly enduring. I realised that what we see on the surface often tells only a fraction of the story. Beneath it lies an intricate web of struggles and resilience, hidden from view.

My mom, who is probably my favourite person in the world, has taught me so much. Despite her own battles, she remained a beacon of strength for our family. Together, we were simply trying to get through each day. At one point, due to various changes in circumstances, we became homeless. Perspective became essential during that time. I slept on various beds and couches, and yet my mom, even while fighting her own battles, was my dandelion, a source of hope and resilience.

Both of my parents had their own struggles, and I've come to understand through those experiences that everyone is facing something. Often, people are unaware of the depth of their own challenges, let alone how they might affect others. This realisation has shaped me profoundly, teaching me empathy and the importance of not taking things personally. Life's difficulties are rarely about us alone; they are about everyone navigating their own journeys.

I wouldn't change anything about what happened during those years. Those experiences shaped me and taught me invaluable lessons. Like weeds, which are often seen as undesirable, life's less-than-pretty moments hold their own importance. They teach us, help us grow, and push us to see the world differently.

Perspective is powerful. Let's rethink how we view weeds—and our negative experiences. They are not obstacles to be removed but integral parts of our growth, offering lessons and strength along the way.

Journeying with Courage

Dandelion seeds, carried miles away by the wind, are adventurers at heart. They have journeyed far from their Eurasian origins, now flourishing across continents. Their story is a call to adventure, urging us to explore, to be open to new experiences, and to courageously embrace the unknown.

I reached a point where I knew I needed to leave. As much as I wanted to support my family, I also recognised the need to seek more for myself. I was born and raised in South Africa, but the world called to me. I wanted to explore; I wanted more. The question became: How could I make it happen? With a South African passport, travel and working abroad is not easy. Then, I discovered the cruise ship industry. I researched the roles available and realised I needed a skill that would make me indispensable. My mom, in her infinite wisdom, gave me the best advice: "You can do whatever you want. Just make sure you have a trade to fall back on." Like nature's way of grounding us even as we grow and shed, her words became my anchor.

I decided to become a hairdresser. I found a place to do an apprenticeship, worked hard, and set my sights on the cruise ships. Despite being homeless at the time and navigating my family's struggles, I clung to my vision. All I had was a blue suitcase and a dream. That suitcase, though long gone now, remains a powerful visual in my mind, a symbol of resilience and determination. Having a visual is a powerful tool to achieve goals.

With a clear timeline and unwavering focus, I worked relentlessly to achieve my goal. Eventually, I landed an interview and got accepted. At 18 years old, I was terrified yet determined. Flying alone for the first time, with only £50 in my pocket and no phone that worked abroad, I left for London and then America to join the ship. Fear was a constant companion, but so was the conviction that I needed more. Staying where I was would have meant stagnation, and I wasn't willing to accept that.

That leap of faith, terrifying as it was, marked the beginning of a new cycle in my life. Like a dandelion puffball carried by the wind, I let go and allowed myself to soar. It was the start of a journey defined by courage, adaptability, and the willingness to embrace the unknown.

Value in the Unseen

Like a master of adaptation, the dandelion reveals its myriad uses. From root to flower, it serves as a feast for the table, a healer in folk medicine, and even an artist's dye. This unassuming plant enriches the soil, leaving behind a legacy of fertility and life. The dandelion whispers to us: even in our ordinariness, we harbour extraordinary potential and purpose.

Imposter syndrome, that feeling of not belonging, of being a fraud, is something we've all encountered at some point. Even those who radiate confidence likely feel it more often than we imagine. I've been there too. On the ships, in London, even in moments of supposed triumph, I'd catch myself thinking, *Someone's going to pop this bubble. I don't belong here.* But here's the thing I've come to learn, though it took years of reminding myself: *Why not me? Why shouldn't I be here?* Who decides what spaces we are "meant" to occupy? Society? Our upbringing? Our own self-doubt? For me, much of that self-doubt came from years of internalising limiting beliefs, bad habits of thought I wasn't even aware I had.

When I finished my contract on the cruise ships, I left with far more than I came with. Confidence wasn't given to me; it was forged in moments of solitude, fear, and uncertainty. There were times I was completely on my own, without a safety net, and I had to figure out what to do. Those moments taught me resilience. They reminded me of the untapped strength within, a strength we all carry but often overlook. That's the lesson of the dandelion, isn't it? It might seem ordinary, overlooked as a "weed," but its roots run deep. Its name comes from *dent de lion*: the lion's tooth. And like the lion, we each have courage and power within us, waiting to roar. It's in those moments of fear, those *I-don't-know-what-I'm-doing-right-now* moments, that we build the strength we need. But we have to give ourselves the opportunity to step into the unknown. To embrace the discomfort. To trust that even if we stumble, we'll find our footing.

I've always wanted to help others thrive, perhaps because I've stood in that space of uncertainty myself. I know what it feels like to doubt, to yearn for guidance, to need someone to say, *You've got this.* That desire to help others sparked a dream: to become a coach, a therapist, a psychotherapist. At first, even imagining such a path felt audacious. Those voices of doubt crept in again, *How dare you think so big?* But now I ask myself, *How dare I not?*

Dreaming big isn't arrogance; it's courage. It's the moment we let our inner dandelion take root, ready to scatter seeds of possibility into the world. And so, my next journey began.

Rooted in Resilience

The dandelion's persistence is legendary. Chop it down, and it returns with renewed vigour. Its resilience is a metaphor for life's struggles. In its tenacity, we find inspiration to persist and rise again, no matter the setbacks. The dandelion teaches us that resilience is not just survival; it's about thriving in the harshest of circumstances.

My journey didn't begin on the traditional path. When I left high school, my grades weren't stellar, and pursuing university or further studies wasn't straightforward. Looking back, I'm glad it wasn't. I didn't follow the usual script of *"what you're supposed to do"*, instead, I listened to that inner fluff ball urging me to spread my seeds and make the most of what I had. I survived those early years, and for that, I am proud.

At 21, I moved to Scotland. My family stayed behind in South Africa. I started a mobile hairdressing business with little more than determination. I didn't know everything, far from it, but I worked with what I had and figured out the rest as I went. I called HMRC when I didn't understand something, likely annoying them with endless questions. But I persisted. While running my business, I also set my sights on a dream: becoming a psychotherapist. To get there, I used a method that has guided me ever since: I worked backwards. I asked myself, *What's the vision? What do I want to work towards? How do I get there?* That vision became my guiding star.

Visions don't always have to be grand or world changing. Sometimes, they're as simple as maintaining stability in your current life. Like a dandelion releasing its seeds, we need to know where we want to land. And once we know, we can take that leap.

For me, the vision was clear: I wanted to practice art psychotherapy. To achieve that, I needed a master's degree. To get into the master's program, I needed a bachelor's degree. And to get that, I needed the equivalent of Highers. It took me 12 years to achieve that vision, 12 years of study, work, and persistence. My path wasn't traditional or quick, but it was mine. And the experiences I gained along the way made me who I am today. Through it all, I leaned on my strengths: determination, stubbornness, and resourcefulness. My mom's advice to have a trade I could fall back on was invaluable. While pursuing my studies, I continued my mobile hairdressing business, weaving my dream into my reality.

Eventually, that same determination led me to another vision: starting a social enterprise to empower adults with additional support needs, individuals too often overlooked and undervalued by society. At first, many people told me I was crazy. *"It won't work. There's no need for it. You can't do it all."* But I embraced the challenge. The journey was far from easy. But I achieved degrees with flying colours, founded a social enterprise that is now nearing its tenth anniversary, and embarked on other ventures, including a new business and a partnership. None of it would have been possible without resilience, vision, and the willingness to work with what I had.

We're all on different paths. There's no "one way" to get to where we want to be. Like the dandelion, we grow in unexpected places, weather storms, and thrive where others might not think possible. The key is to know your vision, embrace your strengths, and trust in your ability to land where you're meant to.

The Cycle of Growth

Nature teaches us that life moves in cycles: growth, dormancy, renewal, and rest. These rhythms mirror our own lives, as we experience seasons of abundance, moments of letting go, and periods of stillness. Each phase holds its own lessons, yet we often resist them. Sometimes, the lesson doesn't sink in the first time, or even the second. Life has a way of bringing us back to the same cycles, giving us opportunities to learn and grow anew.

I found myself in one of these cycles recently. I was accepted into a young entrepreneur and leadership program in America, a dream opportunity to broaden my career and embrace new challenges. At first, I was ecstatic. But as my departure grew closer, an unexpected anxiety began to bubble up. I couldn't pinpoint why. I was excited, but something in me felt unsettled. Instead of pushing the feeling aside, I sat with it and explored its roots. Slowly, it became clear: memories from a past cycle were resurfacing. Years ago, I had left for America under very different circumstances. At the time, I was escaping a precarious and difficult situation. I didn't know what I was leaving behind, or even if I had a home to return to. The parallels between that experience and my upcoming journey were undeniable. During this time, I was going through difficulties in my home life and marriage. Life had brought me full circle, but this time, I was more prepared.

This is one of life's truths: just because we've faced something before doesn't mean it won't reappear. Challenges resurface not to set us back, but to show us how far we've come. Similar situations may arise, but each time, we gain new perspectives and tools to navigate them. I embraced this cycle, understanding that while the circumstances felt familiar, the learning was entirely new.

One of the greatest lessons I've carried from this experience didn't reveal itself in the moment. Often, we only recognise the lesson much later, after we've lived through it. For me, it was the importance of letting go of ego. It's a humbling process, but one of the most powerful things we can do is put pride aside and simply ask for help. The dandelion's puffball is a beautiful symbol of this cycle. It carries seeds to new places, but in doing so, it must release the past. Like the dandelion, we must learn to let go of what no longer serves us to embrace the journeys ahead. Each cycle is an opportunity to grow stronger, wiser, and more open to the unknown.

Life is a Team Game

Dandelions, often dismissed as weeds, are quiet champions of collaboration and support in the natural world. These 'beneficial weeds' send their deep taproots into the earth, drawing up nutrients that enrich the soil, nourishing the plants around them. Just as dandelions enrich their ecosystems, we thrive when we share resources, collaborate, and embrace the interconnectedness that binds us all.

While I've faced many challenges and found ways to navigate them, I've never truly been alone. Even in moments of isolation, when it felt painfully like I was, I can now see the subtle threads of connection that supported me. Like the dandelion, which may appear to grow alone but often thrives in clusters, we are all part of something bigger. Dandelions feed and nurture others, and in turn, they are nurtured by the world around them. They need bees to pollinate, the soil to anchor them, and the wind to carry their seeds. Like them, we need each other.

That said, asking for help hasn't always been easy for me. There were times when I reached out and was met with rejection, doubt, or even belittlement. It hurt, but it taught me an important lesson: not everyone is in a position to help, and that's okay. I learned to be brave and keep asking. I found my tribe, my people, the ones who showed up when I needed them most. And for every 'no,' I eventually found a 'yes.' Looking back, I know I couldn't have accomplished what I have without my community, my mom, and countless others who were part of my journey. I feel immense gratitude for the role they've played, and I'm excited to see who else will join me in the future.

A key part of this journey has been learning to check in with myself, especially my ego. Letting go of pride and stubbornness hasn't always come easily, but it's been necessary. I've learned to recognise when my ego is holding me back and when it's serving me. Our qualities, like pride, stubbornness, or humility, aren't inherently good or bad. They're tools, and it's about finding balance and knowing when to let go or hold on.

Life truly is a team game. We can't thrive without one another. Sometimes, people come into our lives for a season, playing their part in our story before moving on. Other times, they stay with us for the long haul. And like the cycles of nature, relationships evolve, teaching us something new with each turn. The key is to remain open, to keep finding the right people and to never stop being part of the ecosystem that nurtures us all.

The Next Cycle

This new cycle also brought opportunities to launch another business, an idea that had been quietly rumbling for some time. It took me going across the world to realise that I had been ignoring something essential: my inner fluff ball. I wasn't listening to it, but that's okay. More than okay. It's good to pause and rediscover what truly feeds your soul. Through this journey, I've come to understand that my deepest calling is to support others on their journey of supporting others and to reconnect with their inner fluff ball.

This led me to create Determined Dandelions, a business rooted in the belief that when individuals flourish and are aligned, they inspire others and create a ripple effect of change. My focus is on supporting entrepreneurs in cultivating both personal and business growth on a deeper level. Using a framework inspired by the teachings of nature, and combining therapy with coaching, I provide tailored personal development services that enhance self-awareness, unblock stuckness, and equip entrepreneurs with the tools to lead with confidence and purpose.

And so, like the dandelion, I will keep growing, adapting, and spreading seeds of change wherever the wind takes me. Life is unpredictable, but its cycles of connection, resilience, and transformation remind us of what truly matters: our ability to rise again, to nourish and be nourished, and to thrive even in the unlikeliest of places. Whether we stand alone for a moment or in the midst of a flourishing field, we are all part of something larger: an interconnected ecosystem of growth, support, and possibility. Together, we flourish. I leave you with this poem.

Through the Seasons

I feel the weight, a quiet, sleepy call
Shedding layers, resisting it all
Familiar shadows, a circle, a loop
Am I dying, or lost in this troop?
The frost whispers truths I wish to ignore
A time to be still, yet I crave for more

Oh, a stir beneath, a gentle, sweet glow
My roots reach deeper where strength will grow
I am not dying, I feel the shift
But winter's rest was a fleeting gift
The promise of bloom fills the air
A tender start, fragile yet rare

Yes, I've danced here, I know this light
A season of magic, of joy and delight
The sun lifts me up, I'm no longer stuck
The rhythm of cycles. My fortune, my luck
Like dandelions soaring in the breeze
The world sings of freedom, I move with ease

Let me be brave, to journey with might
To release what was mine, and embrace the night
The leaves fall gently, lessons in hand
Reflecting on truths I now understand
Letting go is the price to renew
In courage, I gather the strength to pursue

I've been here before, this familiar stage
The circle returns, yet I turn the page
What did I learn? What seeds have I sown
What will I change in the cycle I've known
Acceptance blooms as I stand aware
Moving forward, with wisdom to spare

ABOUT THE AUTHOR

Danielle is a creative psychotherapist and entrepreneur, with a love of creativity, a passion for sustainability, and a drive to inspire and empower others. She is currently running a charity and social enterprise that she founded in 2015, which provides personal development opportunities for adults with additional support needs. Danielle is also one of 5 partners leading Dundee Changemakers Hub, where we connect and amplify our city's strength to create sustainability for all. Danielle is also starting another social enterprise with the aim of providing support to leaders, and the makers and shakers of this world to help them continue to inspire and be changemakers. Changemaking can be hard, and burnout happens too often. She has a passion for working with teams and the unconscious, and uses therapeutic processes and themes of nature. Danielle love's hearing stories, and different ways of experiencing the world, and has a passion for sharing these to inspire others.

- https://www.linkedin.com/in/danielle-gaffney-du-plooy/

5

FINDING MYSELF AGAIN

GENNA DELANEY

As I sit here and write this story, I don't know what the future holds....

> "Surrender to the divine flow of life,
> Trust in the wisdom of love and grace"

I have been in business for eighteen years! I'm thinking how did that happen? Where has the time gone? It's been a lot of hard work, blood, sweat, burn out and tears. But I wouldn't change it for the world! Designing and making meaningful jewellery, spreading knowledge, and helping women feel empowered and confident in their own skin is my absolute passion.

Ever since I was a little girl, I always knew that I wanted to do something creative with my hands for my career. I was brought up in the picturesque, coastal town of Largs, known for Nardini's ice cream. I loved playing on the beach, picking up unusually shaped rocks, going to the parks and walking up the hills with the dogs. I was always drawing and making things—creativity was in my bones, despite my parents not wanting me to be creative; they wanted me to get a "proper job", like being an architect or an accountant. "You won't make any money being an artist." I didn't listen to them and wanted to pursue my dreams. My parents were self-employed and used to run a hotel, so they knew how hard it was to run a business and were only trying to protect me. They had brought me up with a really strong work ethic—I had to work for my money and started working in the hotel for them, from when I was 12, cleaning, doing the rooms, waitressing and when old enough, working behind the bar.

My passion for jewellery-making started in 1999. I applied to art school after high school but didn't get in. So I started researching creative courses. I had focused my final year project on jewellery so when I came across an NC jewellery course at Cardonald College, near Glasgow, I thought that would be perfect. I applied and got in.

As soon as I started to learn silversmithing techniques, I knew this was what I wanted to do. I loved the technical and engineering aspects of the course and loved to design pieces that had moving parts. I loved creating bold sculptural pieces that the wearer could interact with, but they also had to be wearable. I won design competitions and achieved my HND in Jewellery and Silversmithing with merits in 2002. I applied for art school but did not get in again.

The HND course was fully design-focused on jewellery, but the art school wanted to see more drawing and painting in my portfolio, so I did a twelve-week night class to bulk up my portfolio and started working in a bank in Glasgow.

I tested the water with my jewellery at some craft markets and worked in a little cupboard in my flat while working at the bank. After completing my portfolio course, I applied to art school again and got direct second-year entry into Duncan of Jordanstone College of Art in Dundee in 2003. I graduated with an honour's degree in Jewellery and Metal design in 2006 and launched my business later that year. I had always thought I would move back to Glasgow, but I had built up a good group of friends. I had moved in with my partner and got offered my studio at WASPS right after graduating so the signs were saying stay in Dundee. I worked part-time as I was starting to launch my business.

Awards and expertise – Gaining recognition in the jewellery trade

At art school, I won a Goldsmiths Precious Metal Bursary Award, and they featured my image for the awards. I was also selected to go on their Getting Started business course in London. I used my business plan to gain start-up funding from Business Gateway and got a loan from Prince's Scottish Youth Business Trust (PSYBT) which included a mentor for three years. I was a member of the Association for Contemporary Jewellery (ACJ), and I was asked to co-ordinate and run the Scottish group which I did for a few years. I joined networking groups and connected with many people. My business progressed fast. I won a Jolomo award in 2011 and was nominated as Best Scottish Artist and Designer in the Royal Variety Awards in 2012, I was a finalist in the Women's Business Awards in 2013 and 2014. I gave up my retail job and began working in Alchemia Studio, a lovely handmade designer jewellery shop in St. Andrews. This allowed me to produce a commercial collection to sell through shops and gave me an insight into what customers were buying. I exhibited at craft and trade fairs throughout the UK and Ireland and had twenty-five outlets that stocked my work. I was invited as a guest VIP blogger to visit the international trade show Inhorgenta in Munich, which is like the Crufts of the jewellery world, and they paid for me to stay in a swanky hotel in the centre of Munich—it was out of this world. Eventually I gave up working in the jewellery shop as my business progressed.

Constantly changing and evolving

I was always changing and evolving and moving with the times. I lived and breathed my jewellery business and worked into the night. Now being a jeweller isn't just about making pretty pieces; it meant that I had to become a photographer, a marketer, a blogger, a website designer, an accountant, etc. I was constantly tired and had burnt myself out. I got diagnosed with an under-active thyroid and was told to go on pills for the rest of my life. It really affected my mental health. My body was very sensitive to any drugs, but my doctor insisted I had to go on them. I had also come out of a very controlling and manipulating eight-year relationship with someone who tried to convince me that my business was a success because of him helping me with my website and I wouldn't be able to manage it on my own. I got out of that relationship and got a mortgage on my own while running my business full-time. I had international students coming to work for me over the summer holidays and started to take on part time and freelance staff when the workload was high. They did some marketing, helped make some of my jewellery for my shows and helped me exhibit at my fairs.

Refocus

I had a business mentor who looked at my figures and even though I was constantly working flat out, I wasn't making much money. We looked at reducing my galleries and focused more on my passion for making bespoke pieces of art, marketing my commissions and jewellery classes to get direct customers. My pieces are individual pieces of art which are lovingly handmade. I had been so caught up in running my business, bringing in the bread-and-butter money, that I had forgotten to have fun and be an artist. It had been ages since I'd just had a play in the studio. I wanted to design a new sculptural collection that was different to everything that I'd done before.

I had found a new partner who was younger than me. He was much more relaxed and chilled. He helped me have a better work-life balance. The first few years of dating we travelled, visited art galleries, went to gigs. It had been over nine years since I'd had a holiday, so this was exactly what I needed.

In 2015 I launched a Kickstarter crowdfunding campaign to raise money to buy 3D printing software to design a new wearable art collection, getting back to the roots of why I started making jewellery. The campaign was a success, and I was able to buy the software and mouse to create this new collection. I mixed science, art and new technology to produce bold statement, architectural shapes that I wasn't able to make by hand. I made these from a lightweight, durable material, and as I didn't want the handmade skills to be lost, I incorporated my handmade silver elements and stone settings to add that bit of luxury. These large statement pieces were featured at Dundee Fashion Week and were showcased on models at the Caird Hall in Dundee, and I was in a film about Dundee Fashion Week.

Having a studio at WASPS made me realise that I liked being part of a community—I enjoyed helping others and passing on knowledge. I volunteered for PSYBT mentoring and helped mentor a few young people to set up their creative businesses. I also went to primary schools, colleges and art school and shared my story about how to get into a creative career and running a business.

In 2018, I started an Elevator course. I wanted to focus on how I could push and grow my business further. I had the idea to open my Creative hub which incorporated a retail space, workshop and gallery with a coffee shop and co-working environment to help support other businesses. We would all work together as a team, sharing costs and workload in the shop, and we could host our own individual classes and have time in our own studios and sell our work in the gallery. I presented the idea to the business mentors on the course, but they said I wouldn't get investment or make money from a social enterprise project. Another idea I had was to focus on selling high-end pieces of wearable art. But it didn't know how to get into that market and didn't have contacts. They pivoted my idea and suggested selling my pieces for £30,000. I came out of the course and wasn't sure how to push my business forward on my own. I didn't want to get investment then sell my business, as making jewellery is my passion and I never want to stop creating.

Becoming a mum – change of priorities

Shortly after this, I fell pregnant and had my daughter in 2019, and we moved to Tayport. Becoming a mum completely changed my life. I had lived and breathed my business and was the main earner. All my attention was put into nurturing and looking after my daughter. I enjoyed the early years going to the baby groups, meeting up with other mums for coffee and cake. Being a mum is the hardest, but most rewarding thing I have done. But in the back of my mind, I was always thinking, *how am I going to be able to run my business and be a mum at the same time? Can I still have my studio at WASPS, or will I work from home? Is it professional working from home?* Most of the other mums worked for a company so they knew they had a wage to get back to. Then just as I was thinking of coming back from maternity leave, COVID hit. My garden studio had been built a week before we went into lockdown. WASPS told us we only had twelve hours to go into the building to get our things, then we wouldn't have access to any of our studios. So I dismantled all my tools and machinery and brought all my stock home. But I didn't have the building supplies to build my work benches, so my garden studio sat empty for many months. I had seen other creatives posting on social media about how creative they had been working from home. But I couldn't do anything. I was looking after my daughter while my husband worked through COVID. I had missed time to myself and time for my own creative headspace, but when I was in the studio, I felt guilty for not looking after my daughter.

COVID continued and I still couldn't do much with my business; I couldn't meet clients face to face; craft fairs were cancelled. I had to think about how I could sell my work online and started doing more social media to see if I could get sales. Most of my income came from being face to face with my clients—it was so difficult selling jewellery online. Images just didn't show off the work properly; people needed to touch and try on the pieces. So I started modelling the pieces myself and posted up videos of wearing my collections.

Things happen for a reason. Nurturing my daughter was so important when she was young and as I couldn't focus on my business due to COVID, we tried for another baby. I fell pregnant, but this pregnancy was so different. I felt so ill and kept telling the midwife, but she said it was normal pregnancy symptoms.

It was a regular Thursday, fortnightly check-up with the midwife. I was thirty-four weeks pregnant; our baby boy was due four weeks later. But I felt a bit strange that morning. As the midwife began to check on me, she suddenly said, "I'm so sorry but I can't hear a heartbeat. It might just be the way he's lying, but I want you to head up to Ninewells to double-check." At that moment, I knew everything was going to change. I was in total shock.

I phoned my husband to take me straight to the hospital. My husband couldn't quite believe it. There was a lot of waiting then lots of scans and many doctors came in to confirm our nightmare. My life was turned upside down. Our hopes and dreams for the future were shattered. I felt like I had let my husband and mother-in-law down. To make matters worse it was our daughter's first proper birthday party two days later. She had never had a proper one due to COVID. We'd hired a hall, invited lots of her friends and had to message everyone to say the party was cancelled, while in hospital.

Our baby boy was stillborn at thirty-four weeks. We stayed overnight and saw him the next morning. We had lots of support from the hospital, midwives and health visitors and were able to speak with a bereavement counsellor. We even had a funeral. The doctors found out that I had a rare condition that produces blood clots in the body, so if I fell pregnant again, I would need to take injections for eight months of the pregnancy. This worried me.

We were in shock for months. Everything felt so surreal. My husband was able to get quite a few months off work. We spent it, the three of us together, going for days out with our daughter and spending real family time and appreciating what we have. Grief is so hard. It can hit you at any time, but you have to allow the emotions to flow.

It was coming up to our one-year anniversary of losing Nathan, our baby boy. I had realised I had put on so much weight. I had no energy and no appetite; my hormones were all over the place and I felt horrendous. I went to the doctor who suggested going on antidepressants, but I knew my body and knew that would not help me. I was very sensitive to drugs and wanted to go down a more holistic, natural approach to find the route cause. It was then that I took my health into my own hands and started my wellness journey focusing on exercise, eating healthy and working on having a positive mindset. I had been doing yoga and meditation for quite a few years and continued to practice while I was pregnant with my daughter so it was easy to start incorporating it into my routine again. I put so much work, focusing on myself and my health and started to feel like myself again. After fourteen months of my wellness journey, I fell pregnant again. But I went for an early scan at nine weeks and the midwife told me it was not going to be a viable pregnancy. *I'm not seeing what I need to see here. No sympathy, no bedside manner.* They then asked me to come back in two weeks to double-check that the baby wasn't growing and have the procedure.

My husband and I were in shock again. But this time we got no support. We were made to feel that we couldn't talk about it or acknowledge the loss. It was so early, and it happens to so many people. But women shouldn't just be papped off and left to just go back to work and act like we were never pregnant. With Nathan, I was able to talk freely, cry, let out emotion, but this time round I wasn't able to release. So making jewellery was the only way I could express myself and process the grief.

I have come from both sides of pregnancy loss and the lack of support around early miscarriage/pregnancy loss is appalling. It doesn't matter how long you were pregnant; you still had a baby growing inside of you and there should be support. I am so thankful that I still had contact with my bereavement counsellor, but I felt guilty to speak to her as I wouldn't have got the help if I hadn't lost Nathan first. Because of the way the midwife treated me at the early scan, I felt ashamed, I couldn't talk about it because it was such an early loss. It took six months before I could open up about it.

I don't want other women to feel the way I was made to feel. Women should be supported and encouraged to talk about our losses, at all stages of pregnancy loss. So in September 2024, my husband and I decided to do the 100k walk for Sands to help raise money so that there can be more support and counsellors for early pregnancy loss. We raised £823.70.

Grief is so hard. I lost myself and my confidence. I found it hard to find the joy in life again. For ages, I was focusing on my losses and trying to have another baby. But as I released the grief of the second loss, I started to realise that I didn't want another baby. I wanted to focus on my healing and finding myself and my purpose in life again.

I needed to connect with that little girl who loved to pick up rocks on the beach. Who had so much passion and creativity.

It's really difficult to talk about the loss of a baby, but when you share your story, you find out that you are not alone and you can get through it, one day at a time. Making jewellery has been so good for my mental health and my own art therapy.

I started sharing my story and wellness journey on my social media platforms. It brought me to making jewellery to represent my clients' loss of a loved one.

Working in the garden studio is connecting me to nature. I've started to source Scottish gemstones from the beach and land around me. I love revamping, melting down, reusing heirloom jewellery and turning it into my clients' individual style. These meaningful bespoke pieces allow my clients to carry their memories forever. I've started going down a more spiritual journey and am drawn to healing gemstones in my work. I have always used unusual gemstones with natural inclusions in them but am looking at them with a deeper understanding. I now make a series of healing mantra bracelets, inspired by I Am Affirmations. Your own mantras and words are hidden in the inside of the bracelet for only you to see.

I have been running my own jewellery classes for many years. I really enjoy passing on the knowledge of handmade skills. A lot of jewellery is mass-produced, but hand-making a special piece, just for you, is so special. Making jewellery is like therapy and helped me through my miscarriage when I wasn't able to speak about it. So I now offer jewellery classes as art therapy, get lost in the moment for a day and share your grief if you want to talk about it.

My jewellery business now combines wellness, wellbeing, mental health, educating people and helping empower women to feel confident in their own skin again despite their traumas.

Working on your own is isolating. I want to work with more women and help build a community to bring each other up, grow in confidence and support one another.

I am passionate about

-Designing and creating meaningful jewellery so you can feel comforted and can carry your memories with you forever

-Spreading the knowledge of handmade jewellery skills

-Supporting you in getting into a creative career

-Creating a safe space in my jewellery classes so that you feel guided and supported through your creative healing journey

> "It takes an inner dark to rekindle the fire burning in you
> Ignite the fire within you,
> You need never feel broken again
> Sometimes, darkness can show you the light."
>
> — DISTURBED, THE LIGHT

I still have so much to give to the world. I am transforming and this is just the start of my new chapter.

ABOUT THE AUTHOR

Genna Delaney is an award winning Scottish jewellery artist, who has been in business for 18 years. She produces edgy, architectural pieces inspired by rock-formations and textures from the natural world. Living beside the sea and forest has made her become more environmentally focused, using recycled precious metals, and ethically sourced rare gemstones. Genna is passionate about helping women feel confident in their individual style. She specialises in designing and making bespoke commissions, including revamping old sentimental pieces of jewellery, alternative wedding and engagement rings, and bold statement pieces. Genna loves to pass on knowledge, enjoys working with other women to help them speak about past traumas and teaches jewellery classes in her studio. High profile figures such as Jenny Campbell (Dragon's Den), Judy Murray (tennis coach) and local MSPs wear her jewellery. Genna wants women to feel empowered wearing meaningful pieces of art. She works from her garden studio and lives with her husband and daughter in Tayport, Fife.

- https://gennadelaney.com/

6

DON'T BE AFRAID OF CHANGE

JEN CADGER

To my family – without you, there would be no story to tell and no *why* for the next chapter.

Introduction

Do you ever wake up and wonder how you got here? Not in an existential 'does God exist' way; more like 'wow, the years have flown by. A lot has happened, but I'm not sure I'm really happy or content'.

That was me in 2019. I was 39.

To most observers, I was living a good life—happily married, two great kids, a comfortable home and a profession that I loved. You could say I 'had it all'.

But the reality was a little different. I was restless. I wanted more from life. I felt I was surviving, rather than thriving. There didn't seem to be much joy in daily life or excitement for the future.

I was stuck and a little lost, and I knew change was needed.

Change hasn't happened overnight—it's been a journey of exploration, acceptance, self-development and gratitude. And that journey is ongoing. But I no longer feel stuck or lost. I'm more content in the present and excited for the future.

The early years

I loved school and learning. I've a vivid memory from high school when I was introduced to goal setting. I was asked to consider my future life in one-, five- and ten-years' time. I wrote down my thoughts and popped them into an envelope. The teacher asked us to take the envelope home and open it in a year. Most pupils chucked it in the bin, laughing at the exercise. I kept mine and opened it a year later. I repeated that process for many years, well into my 20s.

Research suggests that writing down your goals makes you more likely to achieve them. I genuinely believe there's something in that. And many of the things I noted down were dutifully scored off the paper. But it also focuses on achievement and looking to the future, instead of feeling grateful, content or living in the moment. It can lead you to a checklist of ideals where you miss out on opportunities or experiences that aren't written down.

My parents met and married quickly, with quite different backgrounds and life experiences—the stereotypes of working class and middle class—which meant, growing up, I saw some of the poorest parts of Glasgow and knew what it meant to struggle to pay your bills. But I also got invited to travel in Europe for passing my exams. And I had a bunch of cousins that lived in London and attended prestigious private schools.

I think my parents loved each other, but I'm not sure they really knew each other. While some couples grow and develop together, my parents grew apart, and their relationship deteriorated. By the time I was 12, it was just my mum, sister and me in the house. It was a close yet intense relationship between the three of us. My dad stayed close by but was rarely present or engaged. There was no joint custody or co-parenting. I didn't really talk about it, even with my closest friends. In the 80s and 90s, separation and divorce still carried a fair bit of stigma and wasn't commonplace.

I was brought up in a semi-rural part of Scotland with fond memories of Enid Blyton-style adventures—cycling to the next village with friends for a picnic, fishing in the local river and the excitement of visiting 'the big city' (Edinburgh!) to stock up before school restarted. It was a simple life with happy moments, but I'd also seen life beyond the town and was keen to move on and explore.

I had an unusual mix of people, situations, contradictions and emotions in those early years. I think I had a broader view of the world than most kids my age, and I had to grow up quickly. But I often felt I didn't fit into the environment around me. I also defaulted to 'fixer' within my family. When there was a problem or issue, I'd jump in and try to resolve it. I felt a huge amount of responsibility and was desperate to keep everyone happy. I developed an unrealistic view of the 'perfect' family, shaped by my wishful thinking and hopes that my parents may get back together. It also skewed my view of what a healthy relationship (whether with a partner, friends or family) looked like, which didn't serve me well.

I studied Politics and International Relations at university, and this was my first taste of genuine freedom. My family was at arm's length, and I had more opportunity to discover who I was. Plus, I got to learn, grow and meet new people—a very diverse group of people, often with opposing views and an interesting take on the world! I saw university as a means to an end—a way of getting a decent job and salary, enabling me to buy my own home. Back in the 90s, that was a realistic outcome.

I bought my first house in Edinburgh at 23—a tiny flat that needed some TLC but became my sanctuary for several years. In my 20s I wanted security and stability, but I knew that lifestyle wasn't guaranteed. So, I wasn't afraid of working hard and I took the opportunities that came my way. I was pretty focused and driven.

While this sounds positive, I developed behaviours that were less helpful. For example, people-pleasing, saying 'yes' to anything, a competitive streak and being far too influenced by others. I lost sight of what *I* really wanted or needed and got caught in the trap of what I 'should' or 'could' do.

For ten years I worked in a male-dominated industry, which had its pros and cons in the 2000s! It's significantly different now; I know that because my husband and closest friends still work in that sector.

Financial Services was a great grounding for a marketing career though. I was involved in lots of different projects and campaigns with decent budgets. I worked with numerous agencies and got the opportunity to run with many of my own ideas. However, it began to lose its appeal once I had my first child. I realised it wasn't very flexible and child-friendly, and the culture was shaped by mostly white, middle-aged men!

The mummy years

Growing up, I was led to believe I could 'have it all'—these were definitely the buzzwords of my generation, especially as a woman. But my honest view is that we can't have (or do!) it all. Rarely are all aspects of our lives in balance at the same time. Show me a woman who has a thriving career without significant help or support around childcare and domestics. Equally, I've yet to find a woman who's 100% comfortable being a stay-at-home mum and doesn't have some thoughts about what they'd like to do when their child goes to school or leaves home. If you genuinely fall into either camp, I think you're fortunate. I fell into the middle ground and felt pulled in all directions with lots of confusion, guilt and self-doubt.

I always wanted to have children, but I didn't have much of a reference point. There weren't many babies in my extended family, and I was the first of my friend group to get married and even consider having children. Whilst I am very grateful for a quick and straightforward journey to having children, I was unprepared for the impact of motherhood. It turned my somewhat planned and organised life upside down. It also coincided with hitting 30 and achieving all the goals I'd set out in high school! I was out of my comfort zone and felt quite lost. I wasn't sure what happened next. At times, I felt really lonely without much support nearby.

That said, I love being a mum. It's given me some of the best memories and experiences in my life. It's also been the greatest insight into my own character and what makes me tick. But it's hard. There's no blueprint. And the amount of love you have for your children can be met with similar amounts of dislike, frustration and anger, especially as they hit teenage years.

I loved both my maternity leaves, each quite different with over five years between them. I think they gave me 'permission' to focus on just one aspect of my life and not feel I had to achieve or aspire to more. There was some relief and ease in that. But having children also kickstarted a decade of trying to find the nirvana of 'work-life balance'. It's an aspiration that I'm not sure truly exists, although I'm closer now than I've ever been. Perhaps flexibility, freedom and autonomy are more realistic outcomes.

I went through several work options including full time employee, part time employee, stay-at-home mum, job share, running a 'family-friendly franchise' (ironically that interview was the only time I was asked if I was planning to have more children!), retraining and changing career. I learnt a lot along the way but still didn't reach an endpoint that felt right or complete. I often felt restless and discontent. However, each move did take me closer to where I am now, and I'm grateful for that journey.

There were times I felt resentful as my husband's career flourished (who accepts a big promotion when their wife is seven or eight months pregnant with their second child without checking in first!). I knew there'd be a fair bit of travel and working late nights whilst I was dealing with a newborn and one at primary school. I definitely felt the gender inequality and the impact of being a woman in a two-profession household with kids. It was a point in our marriage where we had to work hard on our relationship—but we came out the other side stronger.

Amsterdam and the COVID years

By 2019, I was reflecting on some of the choices I'd made and experiences I'd had in life. I was questioning whether I was really happy or content. I was considering (unsuccessfully!) my goals for the next stage of my life. I was feeling restless and not loving my job. Perhaps it was a mid-life crisis. Whatever the reasons, I decided to turn 40 in Amsterdam with my husband and two kids and make the most of the milestone!

It's a trip I'll never forget, and it was the catalyst I didn't know I needed. The city was alive and inspiring, with so many different cultures, beliefs and people. For the first time in a long time, I felt enthusiastic and motivated. Walking along the cobbled streets, I became aware of people working and living differently, on their own terms, encouraged by entrepreneurship and small business development. It felt positive and aspirational.

I returned from Amsterdam and handed in my notice at work. A few weeks later (just as I was set to explore and focus on my next steps) COVID hit.

Fast forward nine months and my new job was 'teacher' to my two kids. Not a bad job, and I was very fortunate to not have to juggle home-school alongside work. But it wasn't easy either. I was applying for jobs, but they were going nowhere. When I got interviews, I might not get a response for weeks and then eventually be told the company was on a recruitment freeze due to COVID.

I remember feeling in limbo and starting to apply for roles that I was only half-interested in. I was really confused and disillusioned, and I shed quite a few tears over those months. I also think my self-confidence took quite a knock. I'm usually good at making decisions. And once I've made a decision, I'm all in. But at this point, I couldn't even make a decision—I had no idea what I wanted and felt really lost. I knew I needed some help, to approach things differently and make changes. I did some local research and found a coach that resonated with me. Coaching became my metaphorical lifesaver, and I benefitted from every session over the next few months.

I went back to basics, getting to know who I was and what made me tick and exploring all possible options. I looked at my values and my future vision. I worked out my priorities and non-negotiables. My self-confidence grew too, when I was looking at what I had achieved, my strengths, my skills etc. I realised I had a lot more to offer than I was giving myself credit for. Until now, I'd not been vulnerable or really spoken to anyone about how I'd been feeling. There was something positive about doing all of this with a stranger and having them support or cheer you on, guiding your reflections and helping you to find answers.

One option that I kept coming back to in my coaching sessions was self-employment. By now I'd worked across different sectors and industries and had amassed nearly twenty years in the marketing profession—but did I know enough to be a consultant and set up my own business? Seeing that question in black and white makes me cringe now. Qualifications: *check*. Knowledge: *check*. Experience: *check*... and I still questioned whether I could do it! Sometimes we can't see what's in front of us.

By the end of my first six coaching sessions, I'd decided to set up Belter Marketing and in between the home school, it was keeping me sane working on something that was just for me during COVID. I decided to embark on more coaching sessions to have some support as I went through those initial few months of setting up my business. It was great to have a sounding board, some guidance, a challenge if needed and someone reminding me of my why and the alignment with my personal values.

By the end of 2020, I'd launched Belter Marketing and had secured my first client. If I hadn't embarked on a coaching journey, I wouldn't be where I am today.

The present

2024 was a big year for me—I crammed in more self-development in that one year than I've amassed in the rest of my life! I became a certified coach and now offer coaching services alongside marketing consultancy. The skills and knowledge I've gained serve me well on so many levels—for my own personal growth, for navigating family relationships and friendships and for supporting my clients.

Marketing consultancy and coaching dovetail extremely well. Often what a client thinks is a marketing issue runs deeper; nine times out of ten it's linked to their personal mindset. Whatever is stopping them from moving forward or taking action, we can work on together. The most common themes tend to be around confidence, knowledge or enjoyment.

I know first-hand how challenging it is to juggle all aspects of our work and personal life, especially as a woman and a mum. If I can help you juggle that more effectively, help you discover a way to thrive rather than survive and help you avoid those feelings of being lost, I'm all in. I'm genuinely invested and will be your biggest supporter. Everyone is unique, and I give my clients a tailored approach that takes account of their work and personal circumstances—the solution might be marketing-related, business-related or something deeper, maybe even a combination of all three.

Don't be afraid of change. Ask for help and let your journey begin.

> "Nothing's going to change if you don't change it."
>
> — DOLLY PARTON

> "Life is 10% what happens to you and 90% how you react to it."
>
> — CHARLES R SWINDALL

My three top learnings from coaching

1. Be yourself

Understand who you are. Self-awareness is a powerful gift and supports all the relationships and interactions you have with others in life and work.

Don't hide your true self. If people don't stay around or choose to move on, don't take it personally; continue to be yourself. You'll find your cheer squad and when you do, look after them well!

Know your why. Get really clear on why you want to change jobs, retrain, set up your own business. This knowledge keeps you focused and motivated, even on the toughest of days.

What does it look like when you're truly being yourself? What are you doing? Who else is around you? How do you feel?

. . .

2. Avoid perfection

Perfection doesn't exist, especially across all aspects of work and life at the same time! Trying to achieve it is a never-ending challenge. Be kinder to yourself and accept that things could be better, that change may be necessary and remember a 7 or 8/10 day is still positive.

The more you do something the better the results or impact. Learning and adapting can take you closer to perfection—lower your expectations when doing something for the first time.

Perfectionism can be a significant block to action, moving forward or making progress.

Consider taking imperfect action and notice what happens. Do you survive? Does anyone else notice the imperfections? What's the outcome?

3. Dream bigger

Don't be afraid to dream bigger or think differently. Our thoughts and beliefs are often so ingrained it prevents us from doing something less ordinary.

Consider some of the greatest entrepreneurs or businesspeople—their ideas tend to push boundaries, expand existing thinking and be disruptive.

Spend time with people who develop or challenge your thinking, adopt a growth mindset and commit to life-long learning.

And remember, dreaming bigger doesn't need to be purely financial, it can tap into your purpose or a passion. In fact, that's often a greater driver or motivator for success.

Take one simple idea and develop it further. For example, a need to help others with their marketing could lead to an online resource hub, to a book, to a series of books, to a speaking tour etc. Visualise as far as you can, even if it starts to feel uncomfortable.

My three top tips for marketing your business

1. Know your customer

By really understanding your customer, you can save yourself time and effort on your marketing. Customer insight can help you to align your messaging to your ideal customers, discover new opportunities and achieve greater impact or results.

Look beyond simple demographics (age, gender, income, education level etc.) and consider a deeper knowledge around how they **think** (their values, beliefs and opinions), what they **feel** (or want to feel) when using your product/service and **do** (the actions or behaviours they might display).

Complete some simple market research with your existing (or potential) customers—a quick phone call or online questionnaire can help you discover more.

2. Nail your messaging

If you're unclear about what you do or offer, then your customers will feel the same. Avoid any confusion and try to be clear, succinct and simple with your messaging. Remember, you should be aiming for the average reading age of a 10- or 11-year-old in your communications and marketing! Having a better understanding of your customers will help to develop your messaging. Be consistent and have the same core messages across all your marketing.

Develop your elevator (or one paragraph) pitch that summarises what you do and how it helps your customers. Highlight three key benefits (not features!) your customers gain from your product or service—try to make these unique to your business.

3. Grow your network and collaborate

No man is an island, as they say. It's unlikely you'll reach success (whatever that means to you) without some help. Grow your network to ensure you have trusted, supportive connections that you can call on when needed—whether that's as a sounding board, to share a specialist skill or to help spread the word about your business. Consider who could be potential collaborators—usually with a similar ideal customer to you—and are willing to partner or work with you for mutual benefit.

Try several networking or support groups (both online or in-person) and then prioritise membership or attendance at just one or two based on a strong combination of:

- alignment to your core values and behaviours
- business and referral opportunities
- potential collaborations and partner work

ABOUT THE AUTHOR

Jen Cadger is a marketing consultant and certified business coach who empowers service-based business owners to master their marketing while navigating work and life effectively. Jen's a Chartered Marketer with over 20 years of professional experience. She specialises in marketing strategy, marketing planning and coaching to develop a tailored outcome for every client.

After a 10-year corporate career in Financial Services, Jen bought and sold a franchise, moved into academia - teaching on the Chartered Institute of Marketing (CIM) professional diploma courses and lecturing in marketing and business management for a number of further and higher education providers. Jen set up Belter Marketing in 2020 and has helped over 50 businesses since. She co-founded Edinburgh Marketing Collective in 2024.

Jen is passionate about lifelong learning, encouraging women in business and youth entrepreneurship.

Jen lives in Edinburgh with her husband, two children and a dog.

- www.beltermarketing.com
- Link to free resources - https://www.beltermarketing.com/resources
- https://www.linkedin.com/in/jencadgerbeltermarketing/

7

FROM LOSS TO LIGHT

BECOMING THE LIGHTHOUSE

KIRSTY MCLEAN

Grief and loss first touched my life at a young age, and their presence has shaped much of my journey ever since. What I couldn't see at the time, however, was that these experiences would ultimately guide me toward my true purpose: helping others heal.

Losing Glen, our beloved Rottweiler, was my first real experience of grief, and at 15 that was devastating. He wasn't just a pet, he was my protector, my comfort, like a brother to me. When the day came to say goodbye to him, I couldn't stay and left before the vet arrived at the house. I told myself it was too painful to stay, but deep down, I was afraid to let my family see me cry. Growing up, I felt I had to be the 'strong' one—the tough big sister. We were a loving family, but emotions weren't openly expressed, and I kept a lot to myself. Strength often meant holding things in and carrying on. I now see how those traits shaped me—not wanting to appear vulnerable and influencing how I coped with life's challenges into adulthood.

When I was 22, my partner of five years Matty, was killed in a motorbike accident in May 2000. Matty had always said to me he didn't think he would live past 30 - he died five days after his 30th birthday. We'd always had a fairly volatile relationship and it had been rocky for some time prior to his passing. Just weeks before his death, we had made the decision to split up. Part of me felt I had no right to grieve for him for this reason, but my head was a complete mess. Some people didn't understand my grief then, or perhaps they couldn't cope with it. So I buried my emotions, telling myself that if I appeared strong on the outside, I might eventually feel strong on the inside. I distracted myself with college and going out partying to try and block some of it out.

Adding to the complexity of that time, I'd had to make one of the hardest decisions of my life: I fell pregnant unexpectedly, but my relationship with Matty was ending. At 22, I didn't feel ready for motherhood and made the heartbreaking decision to have a termination. The experience was deeply traumatic. Apart from my immediate family, who were supportive, there was no real guidance, and counselling was never offered. Looking back, I don't know if I would have accepted it, but I carried so much self-judgment, regret, and guilt. I never really spoke about it. I buried the pain, convincing myself I had to be "strong." But the truth is, the pain stayed with me. Each year on that date, I wonder who that child might have been. For a long time, I felt ashamed even mentioning it—there's still so much stigma around abortion. But if we felt more able to talk about it, perhaps the healing process would be easier. Over time, I've processed it in my own way, but I'll always carry it with me.

Around this time, I discovered Reiki through Elspeth Walker, a Reiki Master and began my training. I would say this was my first conscious experience of spirituality—the start of a spiritual path that would grow deeper over time. I was determined to channel my pain into something positive. I pursued my long-standing interest in Psychology and trained as a psychologist. While I wanted to understand people, a big part of me was also seeking to understand *myself*. I chose to write my undergrad dissertation on Grief & Loss, immersing myself into reading and researching grief.

Over the years, I focused on my studies and lived in various places. Woven into this journey were times of deep loss; the most significant were the deaths of my Granny McLean in 2004 and my Grandad Glendinning in 2013. They were a big part of my life and losing them so suddenly left me struggling to make sense of it all. At the time, distractions helped me avoid confronting the pain of those losses—after my granny passed, I went down to England to pursue my studies and spent a year partying and trying to forget. I later did my postgraduate training in Counselling Psychology in Wolverhampton. During that time, I met many wonderful people, including my dear friend Paul. Paul was a bright light in my life—kind, compassionate, caring, and he had a cheeky sense of humour that lifted my spirits when I felt homesick. Tragically, Paul passed away recently at just 46 years old from Motor Neuron Disease. Paul's funeral featured *The Starfish Poem* by Charles Dale Gray, a piece he had specifically requested. The message of the poem—that even small acts of kindness can make a profound difference—embodies everything Paul stood for. He lived by that ethos, impacting everyone around him in ways that mattered deeply. That sentiment resonates with me profoundly; it reflects my own desire to make a difference in the lives of others. I believe that each of us has the ability to leave a positive mark, no matter how small it might seem.

~

I qualified as a Counselling Psychologist in 2008 and moved up to Angus, Scotland, where my roots are. I continued a long-distance relationship with my partner Iain while I was away studying for years, then in 2012, I found out I was pregnant with my daughter. Even at 35, I didn't feel ready to be a mum and was scared of how much my life would change. I had never been particularly maternal, but I slowly settled into the idea of being a mum. My pregnancy was beautiful, but the birth didn't go as planned. As a self confessed (!) control freak this was difficult to deal with. After 22 hours of labour and hours of pushing, I still couldn't get my daughter out as her head had become stuck. Her heart rate dropped dangerously low, and I was rushed to theatre for emergency forceps. It was traumatic, and I thought I might lose her. Thankfully, she was born safe. I loved her immediately. Unfortunately the birth left me with long term gynaecological issues, which causes me a lot of discomfort and won't ever fully heal. I've carried a lot of anger about how I was treated in the hospital, but over time that's lessened. Becoming a new mum was tough, especially since we had just moved to a new home in a new area. It was also the first time my partner and I had properly lived together, so it was a huge adjustment. I'm sure I had post-natal depression but didn't talk about it, I assumed it was just 'hormones'. I missed parts of my old life and the freedom, but my daughter shaped me in so many ways, teaching me the true meaning of love, selflessness, and what it means to put someone else before yourself.

We wanted to give our daughter a sibling, and in April 2014, I fell pregnant. The due date was around the same time as my daughter's birthday, which felt special. I shared the news with so many people, and I had already started picturing life with another baby. But as the weeks passed, I didn't feel as 'pregnant' as I had with my daughter. At 11 weeks, I started bleeding, and a scan confirmed the baby had died. I was heartbroken. I never thought it would happen to me. I felt so isolated. It was hard telling everyone about the miscarriage. At the time, I didn't know much about miscarriage, and it felt like no one around me talked about it. Lots of people didn't know what to say to me, and I had many unhelpful comments like 'you can try again'. I appreciate people were trying to make me feel better, but it didn't. Over time, as I began to share my experience with more people, I was struck by how many women quietly said, "It happened to me too." Miscarriage is so common, yet so often shrouded in silence. We need to talk about it more, to let those going through it know they're not alone.

Towards the end of that year, I fell pregnant again, but before I could even process it, I miscarried at just five weeks. I was heartbroken—why was this happening again? I'd had such an easy time with my daughter, yet now it felt like my body was letting me down. A few months later, I fell pregnant again, hoping this time would be different. But at seven weeks in May 2016, I miscarried once more. The repeated heartbreak was taking its toll, and I started to wonder if another child just wasn't meant to be. But I became consumed with the idea of trying again and fell pregnant in June 2016. An early scan showed a twin pregnancy—part of me panicked, how could I cope with twins? But I wondered if it was a 'gift' after everything we'd been through. But just days later, I started bleeding.

We had a holiday booked, and not wanting to disappoint my daughter, we went. I told myself to trust the universe, but the bleeding worsened, and the pain became unbearable. Every miscarriage had been hard, but this was the most physically traumatic one. A scan after the holiday confirmed what I already knew—I had lost them. After 14 months of repeated loss and trauma, I told myself that another baby obviously wasn't meant to be and reminded myself how truly blessed we were to have our daughter.

We were referred to an infertility clinic, but I wasn't convinced we'd get answers. Before we even started tests, I fell pregnant again. After so many miscarriages, I couldn't let myself believe it would last. Even when we saw a heartbeat on an early scan, I still prepared for the worst happening. I bled early on and thought, *here we go again*. I was delighted when the pregnancy continued, but it was such an anxious nine months, praying my son would be okay. I went into labour at home, and it was quick, five intense hours. I felt so scared and alone, despite my partner being there. Things escalated so fast I couldn't even make it out of the house to go to hospital, and ended up giving birth on the floor of our study. My parents arrived just minutes before my son was born and mum caught him coming out. A moment that was so incredibly special for both of us, something we'll cherish forever. The paramedics then arrived, and I held my son briefly before I started feeling faint and shaking. I was losing lots of blood but didn't realise I was actually haemorrhaging. I told the paramedics several times something wasn't right, but I didn't feel heard by them. I was rushed to hospital in the ambulance. At the hospital, it all became a blur. I think I dissociated a lot. I have a vivid memory of a Doctor palpating my abdomen to remove the placenta and the pain was excruciating. I was rushed to theatre, and I remember thinking what if I don't wake up? And if I do, what if I have PTSD or can't bond with my son? I spent days in hospital. One of the nurses said to me, "you gave us quite a fright", but it didn't actually hit me how serious things had been until a friend, weeks later, told me that her friend—a nurse on duty that night—said I was very lucky to be alive. It was upsetting to hear that, like catching a glimpse of a reality I hadn't fully faced, a reminder of how fragile and precious life can be.

I spent weeks recovering at home, severely anaemic, dizzy, and fatigued, but I refused a blood transfusion for personal reasons. Just as I was struggling to recover, my uncle passed away suddenly when my son was six weeks old. Despite everything, my bond with my son never wavered, but I knew I wasn't okay - my mental health wasn't good, the trauma lingered and I was signed off work for a few months.

My default was always to 'get on with it' and avoid showing too much emotion—ironic, given that I encourage others to be vulnerable yet struggled to do the same. I returned to work and started therapy for birth trauma, but it led me deeper into why vulnerability felt so hard. Just as I began to unravel things, life threw another curveball. In June 2021, I discovered I was unexpectedly pregnant at 44. I was shocked, and anxious after my last birth experience, I didn't know if I could cope. However, I had only days to process it, and then I miscarried. Given my history and age, it wasn't a shock, but it was still distressing. As always, I pushed through, returning to work, prioritising responsibilities over my own needs. Already juggling two demanding NHS roles, I was exhausted and on the verge of burnout—then I got COVID.

This was the start of my journey with ill health. On July 2nd, 2021, I woke up feeling so unwell and was struggling to breathe. A test confirmed it was COVID. I remember quietly crying in the bathroom. I was so scared for myself and my children. The media chaos and hysteria only fuelled my fear, and I admit I got carried away in it, like many others did. Mindfulness helped me manage my breathing and fortunately I avoided going to hospital. I expected to bounce back, but weeks later, I was still breathless, dizzy and exhausted, but I pushed through because that's what I'd always done. In my job, I encouraged others to honour their needs, yet I wasn't doing the same. I'd tried to be too strong for too long. People urged me to rest, but I resisted, not wanting to let anyone down. Eventually, my mental health declined so much that I had no choice but to be signed off sick. There was a sense of relief, but also guilt and shame around it all. My symptoms persisted, and I was diagnosed with Long COVID. Losing control over my health was overwhelming, and I worried I wouldn't get better. I felt powerless in my own body. I had support from my therapist, family, and friends, but still felt isolated. People often commented on how 'high functioning' I seemed, yet inside, I felt anything but. But that's probably the impression I've always given people. I stayed strong for my children, but I was exhausted. Therapy became a lifeline as I adjusted to my health struggles and a sense of lost identity. At the time, my focus was on getting rid of my symptoms, rather than understanding why they had happened in the first place. I didn't realise then how deeply connected my physical health was to the grief and loss I'd experienced. That realisation became a turning point—the start of a spiritual journey that would change my life.

I was dealing with perimenopause as well as Long Covid, and I attended a menopause event where I discovered Silent Counselling healing modality. I was curious to see if it could help me finally address stuff of the past. I had several sessions with Candice Wilson, Coach and Silent Counselling Tutor and also Marjorie Cooper, Co-Founder of Silent Counselling. The impact was incredible for me. I'd spent years talking about my struggles and trying to heal on a Psychological level but hadn't worked on healing my *body*—so much emotion and energy had been stuck in my body. It was hard being vulnerable and expressing all my emotions, but it was so necessary for my healing. The saying, *"you need to feel in order to heal,"* is so true! Silent Counselling helped me see how trapped I'd been in a victim mindset without even realising it. My body had been holding onto grief and trauma for years, and my miscarriage just a month before COVID had triggered even more—no wonder my lungs (which is the organ linked to grief in Chinese medicine) had taken such a hit. Everything suddenly made sense for me. Silent Counselling felt like the missing link on my healing journey, and I trained to become a Silent Counselling Practitioner. I also reconnected with Reiki around this time doing a refresher course. I went through a profound journey of self-discovery, which I would call my *spiritual awakening* - It was an emotional rollercoaster, but one of my biggest realisations was that- if I hadn't become ill, I would never have done all this deep work on myself. I now see it all happened *for* me, not *to* me. I wouldn't say I'm 'recovered',my healing is ongoing, with ups and downs but I no longer feel like a victim of my health. Having COVID twice more since then set me back again, but it's reinforced just how important it is to prioritize my well-being. I've gotten to know myself on a whole new level and feel more attuned to my needs than ever. To all the wonderful souls who have supported me on this journey—especially Marie Lamont, my shiatsu friend and 'spiritual teacher'—thank you all so much.

After 20 months off sick, I returned to my NHS role, still battling post-COVID symptoms. It wasn't easy, but I'm grateful to still be doing this work. I have wanted to set up my own business for years, and so in June 2024 I officially founded KJM Harmony—a business born from my own healing journey. Every challenge I faced felt like it was leading me here, showing me the power of healing mind, body, and soul. My passion for holistic health runs deep, but my own experiences have made it even more personal. I know what it's like to feel lost in your struggles, and I also know how empowering it is to move through it. Now, I want to help others do the same—to empower them in their own healing journey, and to find balance, peace, and harmony within themselves.

I recently faced another loss—my little guinea pig, Max. He was like my third child and a constant through tough times. Losing him has been heartbreaking. I nursed him for days, hoping I wouldn't have to make that painful decision, but in the end, the kindest thing I could do was let him go, because I loved him so much and couldn't see him suffer anymore. As devastating as it was, it gave me the chance to face something I hadn't been able to when I lost my dog, Glen, years ago. Max helped me open my heart again after years of building walls to protect myself, and for that, I'm deeply grateful to the little soul. Ironically, as I neared the end of writing this chapter, another of our little guinea pigs passed unexpectedly. Grief hit me like a tidal wave once more. It ebbs and flows, but in the pain, I try to find joy and gratitude—because grief means we loved.

Through loss, pain and trauma, I've been guided toward deeper healing and self-discovery. In many ways loss has been a catalyst for my spiritual growth - I've worked hard on transforming my pain into my purpose and my power - not by ignoring the pain but by embracing it and learning from it. At the time, I felt broken, thinking I wouldn't be the same again. But these experiences didn't break me —they *shaped* me, revealing my strength, wisdom, and purpose. Healing isn't about 'fixing' ourselves—there is nothing to 'fix, we are not broken. I believe true healing is a journey of freeing ourselves from the patterns that keep us stuck. I am gradually learning to let go of what I can't control to go with the flow of life, a bit more (it's a work in progress!). Each challenge I've had has been part of my awakening, moving me closer to my spirituality. I've learned that vulnerability, something I resisted most of my life, is strength. It is okay to be vulnerable! Tears are medicine, and feeling is healing. Being vulnerable isn't just for me it's for my children too. I want them to know it's okay to express emotions, so they don't carry the same patterns I did. It's time to step into my authentic self, to be raw, real, and show them that strength lies in feeling. As I've learned, grief isn't something we 'get over, it changes us forever. But it's a passage to move through, not a place to stay. Both joy and sorrow can co-exist.

The work I've done on myself has not only been a 'gift' to myself; it's also a gift to everyone else—my soul mission is to shine my light, to be the 'lighthouse,' illuminating the path for others to grow, heal, and transform.In the darkness we find our own light and when my light increases it creates a positive impact on people around me—the ripple effect. I share my own story in the hope of inspiring others to see that every experience—no matter how painful—can be a catalyst for growth. Pain isn't the end of our story, it can be the beginning of something new. You have the power to tun your pain into purpose.

ABOUT THE AUTHOR

Kirsty is a Chartered Counselling Psychologist with over 20 years' experience in adult mental health. Also a Life Coach and certified Silent Counselling Practitioner, she's dedicated to helping people heal from mental and emotional pain and break free from feeling stuck, overwhelmed, or lost. Working holistically, Kirsty integrates mind, body, and soul to support her clients' well-being and help them reconnect with themselves. She assists clients in uncovering the root cause of their pain and releasing emotional energy held in their body from past stress or trauma. Kirsty is passionate about making a meaningful difference in people's lives, empowering them to create a life aligned with their true selves. A mindfulness meditation enthusiast, she lives in Fife, Scotland, with her two wonderful children and two adorable guinea pigs, who add an extra dose of joy to her days.

- http://www.kirstyjmclean.com
- https://www.linkedin.com/in/kirsty-mclean-8a315943/
- https://www.facebook.com/profile.php?id=100094418057701

8

FROM DREAMS TO REALITY

A JOURNEY OF SELF-DISCOVERY AND REBIRTH

MICHELLE DE ALMEIDA

As a five-year-old I remember twirling around in a tutu and pretending my toys were my children as I played house. Sound familiar?

Throughout my early years, I dreamed about growing up, getting married and having a family. This fairytale did not include my career choice, where my home would be, or how much money I would have. Instead, I could summarise it as "I would be a mother with a wonderful husband and a happy home."

So, how did that young girl's vision of how life was going to be turn into a 40+-year-old overweight woman, who despite professional success felt lost, almost invisible in her own life?

To understand how I became lost, it's important to understand how the human mind works, and if this is you right now, you should know you're not alone; in fact when I opened up about these feelings, I realised it happens to most people at some point.

But those of us who take stock and make a change are very rare. Most people might feel these things at times but the fear of the unknown and what might happen when unpicking their lives is so strong that they stay with the status quo and tell themselves this is just a moment and that they should stick with it.

I think this is a good time to point out that I did get married at a young age (19) to a wonderful man and that I am still very happily married so that part of the story came true. I am truly grateful and blessed to have had his support and love throughout our marriage and we have a far deeper love now as we chase our dreams together.

~

Motherhood and the loss and grief of not achieving it!

Women decide for lots of reasons not to become mothers and I 100% support the right and choice to not pursue motherhood if that's right for you.

As I have shared, as a child it was all I wanted and even through my early teens the feeling and longing to be a mother was with me. So, what changed?

When I was 15, with my first serious boyfriend, I became pregnant and was paralysed with fear. How was I going to tell my parents and what would happen to me?

The then love of my life (I know, very teenage and dramatic) was excited as his own childhood had not gone smoothly and he wanted us to have a family and live together, yet this was not the fantasy I had imagined, and reality was flooding in!

At 11 weeks pregnant, I unfortunately miscarried and as you would expect we were all upset about the loss, although I think some people were probably relieved—and maybe even a small part of me was too.

My desire to be a mother remained but I always imagined I would have time later, and this is when joining the Royal Navy became something I wanted. I aimed to enlist, join officer training and become an accountant because I liked numbers, a story for another time.

There would be time for a family later, right?

I met my now husband in the Channel Islands some years later, and having married my now husband young, we agreed to wait for a family—we wanted to build foundations, have holidays and enjoy being together before we became responsible for children.

Throughout my late 20s and early 30s, we experienced miscarriages and becoming a family felt further away than ever before, which caused a sadness in me that I ignored as I threw myself into my career.

When I was 34, we were referred to an IVF clinic for testing. If you have been there, you know how intrusive personally and physically it can be. I was told that I had a fibroid and that it would impact our potential success but that we could still have treatment.

For the first time in a long time, I was excited by the idea that the man I love and I would create a beautiful child together and have a family, my longing to be a mother was greater than ever.

We went back ten months later—I had turned 35 so we were only getting one shot of IVF from the NHS. We had done everything they asked of us. Before commencing the treatment, we would have one more scan to check my womb.

Everything changed... the fibroid had grown to the size of a gala melon and probably weighed around 14 lbs. It was engaged in other organs, and I would need a hysterectomy. NO chance of a baby. We did not have a choice. I was an urgent case and booked in through the company's private health cover within weeks.

Things moved so fast, and the focus was on my health, having surgery and recovering. I had no time to think about the loss of potential parenthood; I needed to focus on being alive.

So, like other tough times I have survived, I placed the emotions in a box for another time and focused on the task, what needed to be done next. My default then was purely practical, so I went along with the plan and kept moving forward.

What I had not expected was the thousands of small cuts that would be made by other people's opinions, thoughts, expectations or judgment over the years that followed and how each time part of me screamed and cried out inside.

I know that other people meant well or at least I hope they did not mean harm, but I have heard it all over the years. Here are some of the nicer ones:

- You obviously do not like children as you don't have any!
- You chose a career instead of being a mother, good on you.
- Do you plan on having children in the future?
- Can you and your husband not have children?
- Not every woman is cut out to be a mother.

Even the question "do you have children?" can be an incredibly painful one when you first meet people. For their benefit, you do not want to reply "I can't have children" so you end up just saying "no" and moving the conversation on quickly.

My deep desire to become a mother never left me; now thankfully it's a dull ache but for years it remained a physical and deep pain.

How mindset created clarity and simplicity

In early 2021 I had realised I was lost but was unsure how to find myself. I connected with a mindset coach, and he worked through the following questions with me.

- What do you want to do, be?
- How do you want to live your life?
- If you wrote a screenplay of your life, are you the main character or an extra?
- Whose life are you living?

These are the questions that changed everything... the problem was that when I had asked them, I was already past 40 years of age and I realised I didn't know the answers.

I have been on a journey of self-discovery and become a business coach, and the answers to these questions

- What does success look like for you?
- How do you want to spend your time?
- What brings joy to your life and work/business?

form part of my onboarding session with clients, and often they are initially unsure of the answers too!

To understand how you get into your 40s without really knowing what you want and who you are, it's important to understand how our minds work, and how societal norms and good intentions define us all from an early age.

From conception through to the age of seven or eight years old our subconscious mind is absorbing everything around us from our family, friends, TV, video games, etc. and it forms our belief programming.

Things like...

"Money does not grow on trees"

"I am working hard to pay for the roof over your head"

"Get a good job and you've made it!

So as a young girl dreaming of being a mother and having a happy family home came from seeing my parents work hard to provide that for us. I did not think to question *is it what I really want*; I was essentially conditioned to want it.

Now as a grown up I really needed to look at what I wanted and who I wanted to be.

I worked through the questions over the next ten months, while completing a mentorship program with a coach.

Fundamentally I decided...

• Throughout my career I have loved helping others succeed and that this was a personal and professional value for me.

• That I wanted to be wealthy (Health, Money, Mind)

• Gratitude and abundance were now part of my DNA

• I have an entrepreneurial mind that was seeking expression, so I needed to become self-employed.

• Trading time for money was no longer making me happy.

• I was no longer going to silence my own voice.

MDA Business Coaching was launched in December 2021 and at the time the decision was painful as I lost friends, and I caused short-term challenges for my family but now I can look back and see it was the making of me. I was betting on myself, my ability, and the risk has paid off.

I am often asked what I would have done if it had not worked out and my answer remains the same:

"I have a clear goal and destination. The plan of HOW might have changed but the WHERE remains"

I no longer have to have all the answers; I just have to trust that what I need, whether it is money, people, resources, etc. will all become clear to me when they are needed, my only requirements are...

- Belief in myself and my own internal abilities to manage whatever comes my way.
- Determination to keep moving forward, and a commitment to take actions that will move me towards my goals.
- A willingness to be open to opportunities.

Everything I need to create the life I truly want with financial freedom, abundance and the ability to choose how I live each day is in my hands.

A few years on I have multiple companies with 6- and 7-figure turnover, and I do not share that to big myself up but to merely give you an insight into how quickly you can change your life. If you want something enough, it is possible.

The safari moment

In April 2024, I explored a deeper understanding of higher intuition as part of my mindset journey and travelled to South Africa on a retreat with a small group of people and our coach.

I had enrolled in the 12-month mentorship program for my coaching business and believed the retreat would bring clarity to my offering and what my purpose is, but what happened was completely unexpected.

After an early morning safari where I had been surrounded by a family of elephants including some very young calves, we headed back to camp for breakfast.

Elephants have always been and remain an animal I greatly admire and feel a deep connection with so that morning had had a profound emotional impact on me.

We settled down to complete a meditation with the aim of writing down afterwards whatever came up for us.

I was not prepared in any way for what happened.

I wrote, **"In 50 years I will be gone and what will I have left on the planet, what is my legacy, what is the point of my life, of my having lived".**

I had not thought of this at any other time but the sadness I had locked away about not being a mother and not building a family and creating a legacy washed over me.

I went out to the car park to try and catch my breath; I felt like I was drowning. I took deep breaths to stop myself from crying and calm myself. My body was physically shaking.

I felt like I had myself under control and walked back towards the group. My coach asked me if I was ok, and it broke me... a tear ran down my cheek and I said, "no, I don't think I am. I need to go back to my lodge".

He walked me back and offered to sit and listen but I was not ready. I did not understand what I was feeling. I just felt out of control.

Left with my own thoughts I lay down, and suddenly a deep sobbing and waves of emotion and shaking took over.

I do not know what caused this breakdown or how it occurred, but I do know several months on that it was needed. I continue to work on what it meant, healing myself and allowing others to help me understand and forgive myself.

But within months of the event, a deep pain that I had carried in my chest and that had felt like a weight was gone. In its place is an ache and a calmness that I am still becoming familiar with.

I believe I will be a mother in a different way now, not through blood but through the provision of education, leadership and creating safe spaces for young children who have been forgotten and lost in a broken system.

This feeling has created a greater drive in me to be successful; to build financial wealth so I can deliver more impact and ultimately create my legacy.

Delving into spirituality

Having undergone so much emotional challenge in 2024, I connected again with a feeling of wanting to understand myself more.

I am not religious, but I do believe in universal energy and the power of the Universe, so I have been exploring more about astrology and angels and completing life readings along with various ceremonies.

It is early in my journey, but I do believe that I am being guided to continue learning and connecting with this part of myself to complement my more practical strategic nature.

I am excited to see how this develops over 2025 and beyond.

Creating freedom of choice, thought and following your own path

As I am typing this, I am feeling grateful for everything that has brought me to this point in my life. I would not change anything, every event, including the things that have been difficult, because I am today who I am because of the life I have lived.

I choose to be a beacon of strength and light, inspiring others to embrace their true power with grace and vulnerability, to find their voice, stand tall and reshape their world.

It is one of my greatest desires that this book, and my chapter, has created some new thinking in you. Perhaps it has inspired you to believe that you have greatness in you—this is something I believe of all of us.

Whatever else it does I hope you know how incredibly unique and special you are and that you are loved.

At MDA Business Coaching, I'm committed to helping entrepreneurs and business owners reclaim control, break free from the overwhelm, and unlock the clarity they need to create the life and business they desire. Through strategic insights, fearless action, and unwavering accountability, we can turn obstacles into opportunities and transform their journey into one of growth and success.

My coaching programs offer a unique approach that combines deep care with powerful guidance, enabling clients to achieve profound change in their lives and claim their dreams.

Looking back, every challenge and victory has brought me to where I am today, and it's a place of purpose and empowerment. I'm no longer lost but living in alignment with the vision I've crafted for my life and my business.

ABOUT THE AUTHOR

Michelle is a business coach helping ambitious entrepreneurs and SMEs overcome obstacles and achieve sustainable success. With over 20 years of experience across industries like hospitality, retail, and wellbeing, Michelle empowers business owners to take control of their vision, scale confidently, and build high-performing teams. As the founder of MDA Business Coaching, her hands-on approach begins with understanding the heart of each business and its owner's unique journey. Michelle's passion for empowering owners is reflected in her work with programs like Elevator's Accelerator and Coca-Cola's 5by20. She has crafted proven strategies focused on mindset mastery, practical tools, and tailored support to help businesses thrive. Whether you need clarity, accountability, or a growth strategy, Michelle is the partner you need to transform your business and elevate your success

- Website: https://mdabusiness.com
- Socials: @mdabusiness

9

CHOOSING TO BE TRULY ME

RADKA TELYCKOVA

She often complained that the company was all about me. Everyone knew my face, but she felt like she was the one doing the hard work behind the scenes. I told her, "You can do the same. Just show up!" Another recurring frustration was, "You make decisions without me, but this is our company." She often said I wasn't a team player, calling me selfish and claiming I only cared about myself. These conversations came up repeatedly over the years, and they always made me bristle inside.

I've always disliked being told what I'm supposed to do—whether in business or in life. It triggers something in me, a deep frustration I can't ignore. "I need freedom to create, to decide, to follow my instincts", I told her. Being boxed into expectations or told how to act feels suffocating, and it fuels a fire in me.

Jarka was my best friend and business partner, but we parted ways the hard way two years ago. Letting go of someone you love and hoped would stay by your side forever is one of the hardest things to do.

Jarka and I started our consulting company in 2010 after leaving the same hotel where we worked together for three years. We were like twins—tall, striking, and perfectly in sync, both professionally and personally. Our approach to work, especially rate strategies, was so aligned it felt like we'd copied each other. We were soulmates, and I even gave her an armband engraved with 'Sisters by Heart.' I hope she still has it. Though we're on a break, I believe we'll find our way back to each other.

Our journey together wasn't just about building a business; it was about breaking free. We both needed to escape the confines of being employees, stop following someone else's vision, and start doing things our own way. I realized early on that I couldn't stand being told to do something I didn't believe in. Being told what I'm supposed to do makes me furious! Thankfully, my last general manager rarely did that. He trusted me, and I thrived because of it.

Over time, I discovered what I truly loved: trying new things, exploring bold ideas, and carving my own path and helping hoteliers who struggle to see the massive potential of their property. But working as a revenue manager in a hotel often means adhering to strategies set by the hotel or chain, and those restrictions can feel suffocating. After years as an employee, I came to the conclusion that I wasn't made for a role that required me to do the same tasks day in and day out, hit pre-set budgets, and stay silent while generating profits for someone else.

My passion? Independent hotels and small chains. No rigid rules, just spaces where creativity thrives, and strategies fit each property's heartbeat. In these spaces, you don't hear, "That's not how we do it." Instead, you get to ask, "What's possible?"

I cringe at, "That's how we've always done it." That mindset stifles growth. The real magic happens when you challenge the norm, let go of outdated ideas, and dare to try something new. It's about finding your own way, not being blocked by the limits of "this is how we do it."

If you're a hotelier, you probably get it. If you're a guest, know this: behind every polished brand are real people with good days, bad days, and unseen battles. Be human. Just like us.

That's why I launched my podcast, *Behind Every Booking*, in January 2025—to share the heart of hospitality. Because behind every reservation, there's more than just a transaction. There's a dream, a connection, a story waiting to unfold.

After leaving InterContinental Hotels Group in 2010, I realized hospitality isn't about spreadsheets. Sure, strategies and numbers matter, but at its core, hospitality is about people. Leading with heart means embracing what makes each hotel unique, connecting with guests on a deeper level, and letting your energy shine through. And that's where the magic happens because through that energy, you do it your own way—exactly how you feel it and how it feels good and right for you and your business.

This realization didn't happen overnight.

It was a journey shaped by personal experiences and lessons that started long before my consulting career began. It took me many years to understand that doing things "my way" was my greatest strength. Abandoning the need to always be "good" and "loved" was essential—it had been poisoning and suffocating me because I was limiting myself from experiencing what my intuition was screaming at me.

Would I have reached multiple six figures in my mentoring if I hadn't started doing things my own way? No, I wouldn't have. I would have held myself back, prioritizing being "good" for others and seeking their validation. I first learned to apply this lesson at work, and only later was I able to carry it into my personal life. It wasn't easy, though, and I repeatedly found myself in similar situations—different topics, but always the same underlying challenge.

I never met my biological father. Only a few years ago, I found out that I have three more siblings from his family. The man who adopted me left my mom when I was around six. My third father figure stayed until I was about sixteen. I feel sad admitting that I never had that amazing dad who would carry me in his arms and treat me like his little princess.

I only fully realized what this meant after my son was born—that no prince on a white horse was coming to save me. That seeking approval from the men closest to me in hopes that they would love me back... had, in the end, turned me into "a little girl" constantly trying to please.

This realization—about ten years ago—changed everything. First, in my professional life, and later, in my personal life. I stopped trying to please others. I stopped looking for validation. Instead, I started being truly myself.

The puzzle pieces started falling into place, showing me that everything in my life had led me to this exact moment. The path I had created for myself wasn't just a random series of choices; it was a conscious effort to break the patterns that had defined my past.

Let's go back to where it all began...

Where my passion for hospitality started. And where, unknowingly, I had already begun shaping the life I would later fight to create.

It all started when I was nine years old. My family moved to the Czech mountains after the fall of the Berlin Wall to run three mountain lodges. Imagine it: a budget-friendly mountain resort for 150 guests, with ski slopes, an outdoor pool, and endless sports activities. I grew up surrounded by the beauty of nature and the legacy of family-run hospitality. My stepdad always said, "One day, this will be yours."

Many times, you cannot explain why things are as they are. I was not really tempted to overtake the business and work with him. I told him once when I was maybe sixteen or seventeen "I will never respect you". Who knows from where it was coming but I could not help myself.

Maybe... I found out that I can grow more than I could ever think of. At sixteen, I started my internship at the Hotel Intercontinental in Prague. It opened my eyes to a whole new world of hospitality—a world that was just starting to embrace the principles of revenue management. At that time, only a handful of hotels in the region were applying these concepts. Those experiences gave me a unique perspective, but I also realized I needed to step out of my family's shadow to find my own voice.

The lessons I learned growing up in the mountains in the middle of nowhere by the Polish borders and working my way through the hospitality world taught me how to see the potential in every hotel if they follow their own story. It's this vision that I bring to my clients today and this is why they love to work with me. Bringing fresh unconventional ideas to their hotel's doorstep.

It was my life before I consciously accepted the power of "my way"

It was 2010. First, I left my job at the hotel as an employee, and then I got divorced—ending a thirteen-year relationship, including seven years of marriage after realizing I had been living my husband's life, not my own. Again, trying to please him but not chasing my dreams. When I finally acknowledged that the pressure to "have a family" wasn't what I wanted, nor how I wanted to live, I made the decision to leave. We had no kids. It was easy.

That decision brought me to my lowest point. I went through several rounds of family constellation therapy and discovered that I had been living with the mindset of "keeping the peace at home"—which essentially meant "be a good girl" and "don't rock the boat." I had lost sight of my own life, my needs, and what truly mattered to me. I had neglected the joy of living on my own terms, instead of following how others expected me to live. It was a tough decision, but it was necessary.

Two years later everyone kept asking me why I moved to Germany. The truth? It was never my plan or goal. But over time, I realized that, deep down, my subconscious wanted it that way to learn my hardest lesson ever. First I thought I wanted to break free—from being like my mom, whom I love more than anything. Leaving the Czech Republic helped me let go. Out of sight, out of mind.

My second thought was that it was because I needed to meet my son's father. It was because of the love I met. But it was not what I needed to learn. It was not about my mom, my partner or my newly born son at all.

My last "wake-up call" seems almost surreal as I recall it now. In 2017, I broke up with my son's father. He was the one who had convinced me to move to Germany, and at the time, I believed he was the love of my life. Later, I realized that I had projected him as my

Prince Charming and "Missing father figure" —falling into the same pattern, pleasing him to the point of losing myself. How many times in my life had I done this?

Radka, you have to break the cycle, I told myself. I truly felt that now was the time for self-love and for being ME. If I didn't do it, who would?

Tim was just three years old when we separated. I wasn't sure whether I should stay in Germany so Tim could see his father regularly or move back to the Czech Republic, where I had my company and my family. In the end, I decided to try a co-living arrangement. For a time, I lived in a shared flat with a man and his daughter. Tim and I shared a tiny 12 m^2 room that served as our bedroom.

Sharing a flat with another father and his daughter wasn't a big deal—I'm an easy-going person. But what I didn't expect was that this would become the biggest self-love lesson of my life. The final test before I could truly break the cycle.

On the surface, I appeared confident—running a successful company, fully booked as a consultant, and balancing my responsibilities. But inside, I was avoiding parts of myself. Living in that shared space with someone I couldn't stand, a person who was messy and chaotic—the complete opposite of me—forced me to confront my own struggles.

My flatmate was a happy person. He didn't care that the bathroom was disgusting, that the kitchen was a mess every morning and evening. He was totally okay, living his own life the way he liked. And I? I had to clean up first before I could even start cooking for myself and Tim. *How long are you going to accept this, Radka?*

It was like looking into a mirror—reflecting on all the areas of my life where I was playing small, emotionally suppressing my needs. I had spent so much energy being a polished professional that I had completely neglected my own emotional growth.

In my personal life... I was drowning. I was definitely not doing things my way. I was not able to invite friends to this home, to invite my son's friend to play in the afternoon. I was ashamed to tell anyone that I lived in such conditions. It was a tough experience—horrible at times—but it taught me so much. And when I say it changed me, I mean it profoundly transformed me.

Even now, whenever I pass by the place where we lived for those twelve months, I still feel the bitterness of losing myself. Tim remembers it too. He was only four years old when we moved out, but somehow, I believe he sensed my trapped life. Those twelve miserable months were some of the most challenging of my life—but also the most profound in teaching me self-worth and resilience.

Maybe you could say that "breaking up" is my destiny, and perhaps it's not always a good thing. Leaving the problem doesn't always mean solving it. But here's what I know for sure: I have grown more from these experiences than ever before.

Most importantly, I realized that I have nothing to fear. Breaking the cycle of pleasing others and truly discovering who I am and learning to love myself more. And be true to myself in every aspect of my life.

Our paths shape who we are.

We all face moments when we must choose between following the path laid out for us and forging our own. I wasn't interested in inheriting the family business. It's the same with my clients. Every hotel, or any other lodging industry, is unique. Every owner brings their own personality, their own values, their own vision. You can't copy someone else's success. You have to create your own. The best hoteliers are the ones who pour themselves into their work, who care deeply about their guests, and who lead with authenticity.

This lesson hit even more home for me recently during a visit to my grandmother, Vera. She's ninety-one, living alone in a small town near Prague, and facing the challenges of early dementia. When she didn't answer my calls for two days, I drove 450 kilometers from Munich to check on her. I could hear her slippers shuffling behind the door before she opened it. When she saw me, her face lit up with the most beautiful smile.

"Radunko," she said, using the nickname she's called me my whole life, "I'm so happy you're here." Everything felt warm and safe.

Even though she asked me over and over again, "What can I get you?" all I needed was her smile.

That's the essence of hospitality. It lies beyond fancy amenities or cutting-edge technology. It's about the way you make people feel. It's about creating a sense of belonging, of care, of connection. Imagine treating your guests like family—welcoming them with joy, saying goodbye with gratitude, and giving them memories they'll carry forever.

One of my favorite stories is about a boutique hotel owner I worked with in 2018. The hotel had opened just nine months earlier, but they already felt like they were struggling. The hotel manager called me for help. Over two days, we worked together to redefine his vision. I also spent quality time with the hotel owner, a young, very attractive man. While he was clearly charismatic, I advised him to stop focusing on "selling rooms" and instead start telling his story. I could immediately see how successful he could be if he turned his own story, family story into his hotel business. His family had a winemaking heritage, so we built packages around wine tastings and curated guest experiences. Today, he's thriving—not just financially but emotionally. His social media is full of authentic posts that connect deeply with his audience.

That's what I love about this industry. It's not just about revenue and the money-making process; it's about creating something meaningful. It's about leaving a mark on people's hearts. And doing it your own way which will make it even more personal. Your guests will love you for that.

Over the years, I've mastered all the skills of revenue management to help hoteliers. I can analyze data, create budgets, and build complex strategies. But the more I work in this field, the more I realize that success comes from the heart. It comes from showing up every day with the intention of making someone's experience unforgettable. It's about being resilient, staying authentic, and caring deeply.

I've discovered that combining a strong skill set and tools with the right mindset in revenue management creates something extraordinary. This approach is rare in an industry often dominated by exact numbers and rigid strategies, but it's where true innovation lies.

In the end, it all comes down to what you believe, how you feel, and what you've accepted as your truth and reality. As a revenue manager, hotel strategist, and consultant, I've learned that true success begins with mindset.

If you believe your hotel rooms are "too expensive," or that guests won't book because "we don't have a pool like our competitors" or "we don't have money for renovations"—then guess what? You'll always find reasons to justify those limitations. And as a result, those beliefs will become your reality.

Even in business, we must choose our thoughts as carefully as we choose our clothes or the partners we want in our lives. Because what we accept as true will shape every decision we make.

This is a question I hear often, and it highlights the delicate balance between pricing strategies and long-term goals. The key isn't just about what competitors are doing—it's about understanding your unique value, knowing your ideal guest, and crafting a strategy that aligns with your vision for your property.

It's not just about the rate itself; it's about the story that rate tells and the experience it promises. You don't need to lower your rates to attract the right guests; you need to raise your standards—starting with your mindset.

What if we went deeper? What would happen if we began adopting techniques like neuro-linguistic programming (NLP), energetic approaches (raising vibrations), or EFT (emotional freedom techniques) to overcome fears of loss or failure? What if we used these methods to successfully launch direct booking strategies for hoteliers, revisit pricing not based solely on reports but also on intuition and gut feeling, or attract ideal clients through visualization and manifestation?

Some might call this crazy—especially in corporate hospitality settings. Big names in the industry might dismiss the idea of setting prices based on intuition. But for independent hoteliers, this approach is transformative. By combining mindset, skillset, and toolset, you create a powerful synergy that goes beyond conventional strategies. It's no longer just about spreadsheets or formulas; it's about feeling the energy of your business, visualizing success, and believing in the value you offer.

Yes, maybe I'm the only one in the world who includes mindset training in revenue management programs, but I knew it was the missing piece in helping hoteliers grow from within. Stop fearing that a wrong price strategy will kill their business.

So, I gave it a go. I told my client, "I believe this is the right approach. I can't teach you tactics if you're undecided about your goals and relying on me to tell you what to do. This is your hotel. If it were mine, I would be doing X, Y, or Z, but it's not mine. You must take 100% responsibility for your decisions and the results that follow."

Never live the life of others

Choosing to be truly me has shaped how I help my clients—empowering hoteliers to trust their instincts and create their own paths. It's not about copying strategies; it's about aligning decisions with their unique vision. That's why I combine mindset work with skillset and toolset training. Without clarity and confidence, even the best strategies fall flat.

This approach isn't for everyone, and that's okay. But for those ready to take the leap, I've witnessed transformations—not just in revenue but in leadership, team dynamics, and personal growth.

Take my client, who runs a charming chateau hotel in Portugal. After breaking free from his family legacy, embracing a growth mindset, and applying my strategies and tactics, he generated over 100K in one year without a massive technology upgrade. He has just started to become fully aware of the power of mindset work. His plans for 2025? Even bigger—thanks to this revenue increase he's adding three more rooms to his inventory, something he never believed was possible.

Mentorship is at the core of my work. Through weekly sessions and live training, I guide hoteliers to find their own path, not just in business but in life. I become the person to help them move on and remind them often, "If you don't act now, who will?"

When I walk into a hotel, I instantly sense its potential. My role is to ignite that spark within hoteliers, helping them see and believe in their own vision. Passion isn't taught; it's discovered. Not every client sees it, especially after running a hotel for a decade or two. When I come to a hotel, it's like a breath of fresh air. I have my antennas everywhere. In a year, I'm able to work 1:1 with three hotels while also engaging personally with an additional twenty to thirty hotels in group settings. I witness their successes and how they transform their ideas, as well as implement my recommendations and strategies. Over the years, I've seen and experienced so much that, after 25+ years of practice, I can evaluate and identify solutions very quickly and know precisely when to bring them to life. My intention is always honestly sharing what I see (revenue translated into your numbers and KPIs), how I feel about them doing their own business (marketing), and whether the potential is there (mindset to change it). That's why I created the Inevitable Hotel Success Mentorship Programme—combining strategies (skillset), technologies (toolset), and mindset for business growth. The change is coming from within and only you can master it on your terms.

Here's the truth: no strategy works if you're not ready to fully commit to it. And no strategy feels right unless it's aligned with who you are and the vision you're creating. This is why I say, "You don't just run a hotel—you create an experience, a story, and a legacy. The numbers follow when the heart and mind are aligned."

And what's more, true success isn't about following someone else's blueprint. Don't fall into the trap of thinking, *'If this works for them, it will work for me as well.'* Or as my grandma always said, *'If two people do the same thing, it's never the same.'* It's about defining your own path, leading with authenticity, and building a legacy that's unmistakably yours. Your way is the right way. Your success is inevitable and goes beyond numbers and spreadsheets. Only YOU can make it truly yours, aligned with what makes you happy and fulfilled.

Hospitality isn't just a (real estate) business; it's about people, energy, and connection. Behind every booking is a story—a person with dreams, worries, and hopes. Guests bring more than luggage; they carry emotions, expectations, and sometimes their stress. That's the raw, real side of hospitality. It's the same in life—authenticity is the thread that connects us all. I genuinely love showing you that you are strong enough to make it your own, both in business and in life. Because choosing to be truly me isn't just my story; it's an invitation for you to do the same.

ABOUT THE AUTHOR

Radka Telyckova is a hospitality consultant who works with hoteliers and businesses struggling to maximize their profitability and unlock their full potential. She helps them optimize revenue, streamline operations, and embrace bold strategies so they can achieve sustainable growth and lead with confidence. With over 20 years of experience, Radka began her career at just 16 at the Hotel Intercontinental in Prague, witnessing the rise of modern revenue management. In 2010, she co-founded her consulting company, guiding clients across Europe through complex challenges in both business and mindset.

Radka's journey isn't just about numbers and strategies—it's about courage. She left behind a seemingly stable life abroad with her three-year-old son, choosing to start over in a tiny room with a stranger. That bold leap taught her that true success comes from daring to be yourself. She lives in Munich with her son, proving every day that growth begins where comfort ends.

- Radkatelyckova.com
- https://www.linkedin.com/in/radkatelyckova/
- Behind Every Booking Podcast: https://open.spotify.com/show/3dai8rfZU7AneyXIXm9k7t

10

FROM CHASING BUTTERFLIES TO BREAKING OUT OF MY COCOON

RENATA TARI

Sometimes, figuring out who we are takes us on a wild ride back to when we were little kids. For me, it's like hopping on a time machine straight to my days as a little girl. I've always been obsessed with stories—books, to be precise. One of my absolute favourite places in the whole world was the library. To me, it was a treasure island (minus the pirates), full of tales about heroes, adventures, and people who lived lives so different from mine but made me believe I could be one of them one day.

Growing up in a tiny Hungarian village, dreaming about far-off lands and big adventures felt like planning a space trip with a toy rocket. Nobody in my family had ever travelled outside the country. We didn't even go on holiday, besides visiting grandma 300 miles away. Travelling to a foreign country? Unheard of. The closest thing to exotic was visiting my godmother in Budapest. But in my mind, I was already out there, conquering the world, travelling and living across faraway continents and chatting in fluent gibberish with strangers.

Stories were my first love. And my second love? People. Even as a kid, I couldn't resist a good yarn, whether it came from a book or the old ladies on our street. Picture this: every house had a bench out front, and every bench had an old lady on it, knitting, shelling cherries, or swapping gossip. I'd sit with them, nibbling on cake or sipping tea, soaking up their tales like a little sponge. They probably thought I was just there for the snacks (I mean, partly true), but really, I was fascinated by their stories, learning the wisdom and the history of the old days. I loved hearing about dances and how they met their love.

When I wasn't with the ladies, I was off running through cornfields, building bunkers in the forest, or playing ogre wars with the neighbourhood kids. Life in a small village might seem dull, but I turned it into an adventure. Every horse I saw became a steed for a knight, every bug was a magical creature, and every tree held the secrets of a faraway kingdom. My imagination worked overtime, turning the ordinary into the extraordinary.

But life wasn't all tea and cherries. My parents divorced. My mom had the courage to leave my alcoholic, abusive father who did horrible things under the influence of the booze. He struggled with his own demons—mainly the kind found at the bottom of a bottle. I'll always be grateful for my mom's bravery for leaving him. It was one of the first acts of real-life heroism I ever witnessed. It wasn't easy, but I'm forever grateful to her for having the courage to leave. Although my new stepfather (a few years after) wasn't much of a father—from my real dad's physical abuse to psychological warfare—it was a step up; at least I was safe. Physically.

Through it all, that little girl with one hell of an imagination never stopped dreaming. Sure, there were times when life knocked the wind out of me, when curiosity took a backseat, and adventure felt out of reach. But the drive to discover, to learn, and to help others always pulled me back.

Maybe it was all those hours spent listening to the old ladies or playing with my uncle, who had Down syndrome, that made me a natural at connecting with people. While my cousins were too busy being mean to him, I found ways to play, to laugh, and to make him feel seen. Looking back, I think that was my first step toward becoming a healer—someone who listens, who cares, and who helps others find their way.

That little girl with a wild imagination and knack for turning bugs into best friends? She grew up. She faced some tough times, but she never let it break her. If anything, it made her stronger, more determined to write her own story, and more curious about the stories of others.

And you know what? She's still here—just with a little less running around aimlessly and a lot more life experience. But let's see what kind of experiences she had later in life that helped her become who she is today.

A mosaic of moments

It's funny how life is just a mosaic of moments—some sweet, some sour, some bitter, or even bittersweet and some that stick to your heart forever. When I look back, I realize how the tiniest things—offhand comments, awkward encounters, or those accidental moments of kindness—shaped me. The weirdest part? Some memories are sharp as glass, while others are hazy clouds. My childhood? It's more of a hazy cloud. I have a hard time recalling most things from my early childhood, and even later in high school things are hazy, but maybe that's for the best.

They say kids block out the bad memories to cope. Maybe they're right. Sure, I had fun. I had friends. But I also got my fair share of heartbreak—being bullied in primary school for being poor. Kids can be mean and insensitive. They called me a "gypsy" just because we lived in the part of town where most people were gypsies, and I had dark features. It stung though, as I was the *helpful, smart, good-grades-kid*—the one everyone wanted for homework help but mysteriously forgot on playday. I had a few close friends, but loyalty can be slippery, and most of the time I was either the outsider or the leader who looked after everyone. Like it wasn't enough to be responsible at home for my little brother and sister and my mom's emotional breakdowns, responsibility followed me everywhere.

High school was my reboot. It was 50 kilometres away, far enough that no one knew me or my family. For once, I wasn't "the poor kid" —I was just me. Smart. Fun. Helpful. And for the first time, I felt like I could actually *be* myself. But life wasn't all sunshine and study sessions. Back home, things were rocky. My stepfather? Let's just say "supportive" wasn't in his dictionary. If you had someone in your life who is much less intelligent than you, criticizing you all the time for everything you did, you have two options: you break and start believing you're not good enough, or, you disregard everything they say as you know they don't know what they're talking about. I did the latter, but it came with a price—I grew a shield around my mind to not just disregard the bad things he said. Anything anyone said about me, good or bad bounced off my armour. I was who *I* thought I was only my opinion mattered, and as it's usually the case—I became my biggest critic. I did need that armour, living in that house, to fulfil the role I played in the "family", I had no choice but to be tough.

I was the family referee—looking out for my brother, sister, and even my mom, keeping my stepfather's idiocy away from them, focused on me. But where was my safety net? Spoiler: it didn't exist. Maybe that's why I'm so independent now. I've spent years unlearning the "don't ask for help" mindset. Progress? Sure. But I still tend to DIY my way through struggles, armed with books, online courses, and sheer determination.

Turning 18 should've been a milestone, right? Well, it was a big stone for me, I got booted out the morning after my birthday. Yup, my step-dad told me in the morning after my 18th birthday that I spent with my friends that I had two hours to pack my bags and get out. I was shocked, had no money—he gave me no money, nor did my mom. Instead, he accused me of stealing his money. Irony? I got more money in monthly benefits after my father's death than my step-dad brought home as a salary. Anything spent on me? The bare minimum. He was so "intelligent", he couldn't use his own bank card, and my mom often asked me to take money off it. That gave him the perfect excuse to kick me out, accusing me of stealing. However, it wasn't all bad. I had a place to go—my late dad's house up north I inherited, where his parents lived—and I was a certified nurse (yes, back then in Hungary you could get a profession with your high school degree. Wasn't that a nifty thing?). So, 10 days later, I was in a hospital working in the ER, finding my footing and trying not to think of my little brother and sister, of how their life would be without me.

Plans to go back to school? Delayed but not forgotten. Life threw me another curveball: family drama. One year later, my mom ended up in a psychiatric ward. My siblings needed me, and guess who stepped up? Me. Again. But after months of enduring my stepfather's nonsense, I had an epiphany. Loving my family didn't mean setting myself on fire to keep them warm. At 19, I chose *me*.

That choice? Life-changing. I shredded my chains, went back to my house, started to look for different jobs because as great as nursing was, it paid very little, and I couldn't go back to my old job anyway. I explored many options and tried my hand at everything—bartending, hospitality, travelling around Europe, learning languages, and soaking up new cultures. Each twist and turn reshaped me, opened my eyes and made me the smart, resilient, curious, adventurous, cosmopolitan woman I am today. And humble—don't forget humble.

Looking back, I don't blame my past for who I am today. If anything, it's the forge that made me a fighter. Life didn't go as planned, but honestly? It turned out to be a pretty epic ride so far.

Scotland calling

So, how did I end up in Scotland? Honestly, it was a coincidence. I couldn't make this up if I wanted to: I'm in Venezuela, applying for a job in care online via Skype, armed with my long-dormant nursing credentials and a pinch of optimism. I got a role in elderly care, and Edinburgh became my first stop—not because of some cosmic alignment (or was it?) but because the National Insurance appointment in Edinburgh was faster than London's. Go figure.

And you know what? Edinburgh hooked me. I won't pull the cliché "fell in love with the city," but let's just say it had me at "hello." The history, the stunning architecture, the hills, the seaside—it was like someone designed a city using all my favourite things. Not too big, not too small; just what I liked. So, I stayed.

The first couple of years? A mix of care work and side gigs while figuring life out. Eventually, I went back to IT, but Scotland came with its own set of challenges. For starters, the culture shock, especially right after living on a Caribbean Island for a year. I come from a place where "straightforward" was our love language. Here? Let's just say "blunt" wasn't always appreciated. I had to polish my social skills and soften the edges of my honesty—sometimes I still rub off on people as "harsh" or downright "rude", but one can only change so much without losing oneself.

And then there was *the weather*. The first time I got here, I heard this joke: Two Scots are talking. One says, "Last summer was very nice." The other says, "Yes, I remember. It was on a Wednesday." And it's not that much of a joke. After over 10 years here, I definitely see the irony. Long winters without snow felt like a cruel joke, and for the first time in my life, I wrestled with depression. Isolation was a new beast. I've lived abroad before, but making deep connections here? That's a whole other story. People seemed hesitant, like, "How long are you staying? Should I invest in this friendship?" It's still an ongoing challenge. But it can be me, just my charming, somewhat cynical, sarcastic personality.

And then there was COVID. At first, I thrived. Extra hours in the morning? Boom—home workouts. I lost weight, felt amazing, and was practically glowing. But by year two, the shine wore off. I missed people. I missed meaningful connections. And I had a moment of reckoning: I didn't want to keep working in a job that left me cold. Sure, I was good at it, but I only had the mind for it not the heart for it. Cue the existential career crisis, or is it midlife after 40?

Finding and following my calling? Oh, it's been a journey—one fuelled by a stubborn desire to do what I love *on my own terms*. Helping people has always been my thing, whether it was through nursing, tourism, or now, coaching and energy healing. At first, I was stuck in the "I'm not ready yet" phase, aka the "I'm still learning and probably not good enough" rut. Doing courses, reading books, going to seminars, tarot cards, meditation, mindfulness, neuroscience, you name it. I absorbed knowledge like a sponge. But even though I could answer most questions and stand my ground in conversations in advanced coaching environments, I still felt like I didn't know enough.

Then, something snapped me out of it: a company presentation about coaching and mental health. Sounds inspiring, right? Wrong. It was so bland and lifeless that halfway through, I thought, *"Seriously? I could do this—and make it fun!"*

Cue the little voice in my head that wouldn't shut up: *"If you can do it, why aren't you doing it? Do it. DOOO IT. Show me!"* Relentless, that voice. So, I finally listened. I took the leap, launched my own company, built a website, and started building my social media, learning to use nifty AI tools, and hunting for coaching opportunities. I began brainstorming ways to share my vision and promote my business. That leap of faith also opened the door to something I've always loved: writing.

Becoming a writer

Writing has always been woven into my life, but this book? It's special. It's not just a way to flex my coaching and healing skills—it's also fulfilling a dream I've carried for years: to be a writer. So let's talk about writing! Writing has always been my secret life goal. If I can do anything, money not an issue and all, I'd live on a farm, with some animals (maybe a loving husband but that's optional), tending my garden and writing books. I've scribbled poems (one heartbreak-inspired collection did make it to print), short stories, and even half-finished novels. But this time, I felt a pull—a chance to share my story. Maybe my journey, with its twists and turns, could inspire someone else.

So, what have I learned from my journey? Well, for starters, every twist, turn, and slap in the face has shaped me into who I am now. I couldn't help others build strong foundations if I hadn't rebuilt from the wreckage caused by my own decisions. My authenticity—my true self—is my superpower. Science backs me up on this: authenticity is right up there with gratitude and love. Moreover, it gives you a little extra, if you are authentic, nobody can copy you. And that's my mission—to live authentically, unapologetically, and fully as my a-*f*cking-mazing* self.

Am I done learning, evolving, untangling the knots in my psyche, and breaking down barriers to reach my full potential? Hell no, work in progress till the end. Meditation, energy healing, exercise, dance, coaching, self-development, writing—even eating the right foods—are my tools (it sounds like a lot but can be done in 30 minutes to an hour a day). Maybe I'm already closer to my goal than I think. Or maybe I'm exactly where I'm supposed to be. Time will tell, right? The point is, every triumph and every tough break has brought me to this moment, and for that, I'm grateful.

Take being kicked out of my house at 18, for example. Sure, it was rough at the time, but if it hadn't happened, I might still be stuck in that tiny town, living a small, non-story-worthy life. And where's the fun in that? Instead, I've got a chance to write my own story. Literally. One that involves new beginnings in new countries, challenges, adventures, and yes, the occasional "what am I doing with my life?" moments. But here's the upside: starting over? It doesn't scare me anymore; the opposite, I crave it. I've done it so many times, it's practically a routine.

Back in my 20s, I was all about spontaneity—throwing darts at a map (okay, it was just Europe, but still) and heading wherever they landed. Those days were wild, fun, and filled with adventure. Do I regret it? Not for a second. But now, I've traded dart-board decisions for mindful ones. I still don't have a detailed roadmap for the future, but I know where I'm heading. And this time, I'm taking deliberate, thoughtful steps to get there.

What's next? I don't know exactly, but can we ever be sure what the outcome will be? No, but by embracing the messy, thrilling process of building a dream life, life becomes a fun story you write yourself. Because if there's one thing I've learned, it's that the only way to get where you want is to start doing.

Ultimately, I'm chasing a life that lets me reconnect with the little girl I used to be—the one who loved writing, dancing, running through fields, and brushing her hands across flowers as she passed. That girl lived life on her own terms, unbound by rules or expectations, just loving life. And if I could find my inner little daredevil, so can you. I hope my story inspires you to go find her. You got this!

P.S. I recently had a bad experience—not tragic, just someone being mean to me for no reason, totally resistant and with no light in the interaction. It felt hurtful, but after reflecting on it throughout the flight (yes, it was an airport, of course), it gave me an idea. I needed a "card of kindness" to give to her saying, "You need this more than I do". Not to be mean, but perhaps it might have inspired a spark in them to be more open to being nicer to others. So, I decided to start a movement of kindness and a webspace where people could share their stories and be inspired. Although I don't support doing nice things for "likes", I see the benefit in sharing to inspire people to be kinder to each other. Giving is living.

ABOUT THE AUTHOR

Renata Tari is a Life Coach & Spiritual Healer. We each have a unique story and perspective, shaped by our experiences. Even within the same family, the experience is unique. Renata's journey made her a survivor, a fighter, a healer, and a storyteller. The hardships—the broken glass she's walked on—cut her deeply, leaving scars. Some were surface wounds, while others struck deeper, but every scar taught her resilience. Over time, those scars became shields, making her stronger, less vulnerable. Though there is still broken glass on the road, she's learned to swipe it away and even if some still go unnoticed, the pain taught her to navigate life more wisely. That hard-earned knowledge inspired her to create Belle Morph—a space to help others transform pain into beauty, just as Renata has. "Belle Morph" signifies metamorphosis: taking life's wounds and turning them into strength and beauty, so others can gain wisdom without enduring the same pain.

- https://bellemorph.co.uk/

11

NO STORM LASTS FOREVER, BRIGHTER DAYS ALWAYS RETURN

VICKI OSTROWSKI

"I am sorry, madam, that card's also been declined".

The words felt distant, detached.

I stood there on legs that were now so shaky in my Gucci shoes that they could barely support my weight; my hands sweaty, my heart pounding, my throat so dry I couldn't even speak; clutching the purse that matched the shoes in my shaking hands.

It was early morning, and the garage was full of tradesmen, getting coffees and pastries before setting off to work. I felt all of their eyes on me, judging me, feeling sorry for me, even internally laughing at me—look at this crazy lady with all of her expensive stuff, as every single one of my multiple cards was declined for the fuel I had just put in the car on the forecourt, the car that was less than a year old with personalised plates.

Sweat was running down my back, despite it being a cold November morning, and heat radiated from my face and neck. I fought back the urge to burst into tears, as fear, shame and embarrassment consumed me. I felt like I had been sucked into a void with everything going on around me in a parallel universe.

I only wanted to take my children to school, who were sat in the car in anticipation of a normal day ahead, probably singing to songs on the radio like they did most mornings, gratefully oblivious to what was unfolding just meters away.

That day would turn out to be anything but normal.

They say life can change in a heartbeat, and while that's a cliché, I really didn't warrant just how true that was until the words above were uttered and the events that day unfolded.

The Whirlwind

A few years earlier, still young, newly single, single parent to two young children, still in a bit of a daze from my marriage ending, I was swept off my feet!

I wasn't looking for a relationship, that was the last thing on my mind, but here he was the British guy of Italian descent, who told everyone he was Italian; it was a whirlwind.

And just like a literal whirlwind. It sucked me into a tumultuous environment, biding its time before it was ready to dump me back on the ground again at some point in the future.

In the throes of that whirlwind though, something felt off; like the dream that wakes you up, you know it was upsetting but need to scan the recesses of your mind as to why, only to never be sure.

So, as I wasn't sure what that feeling was, I instead told myself that things that felt 'off' were from my previous failed marriage experience and not from this exciting new relationship.

The gifts, the flirty texts, the talk of the future in those first fast weeks, just didn't match with the 'off' feeling.

So, I ignored and learned to silence the feeling in the pit of my stomach that came out to play daily and instead allowed myself to be further pulled into the whirlwind that was my new romance.

As the initial intensity began to subside, I chose to overlook certain behaviours, such as his delayed responses to my calls over several days. I ignored occasions of being stood up for dates, and his refusal to stay at my residence, opting instead to leave after spending time together. I accepted his explanations, considering he had recently ended a challenging relationship too, and when I questioned these occurrences, he advised me to have 'patience' as he was also healing.

The Take That song of the same name was also of a similar time and hearing the song and the lyrics even now makes me inwardly cringe.

There were periods when he was unreachable for days without even a text message, and people informed me of seeing him with someone else. He assured me that it was his cousin and provided detailed explanations about Italian family dynamics, and while I wasn't convinced, I had no viable argument to prove otherwise. There was even one occasion that we had booked a weekend away and he didn't turn up for it, and when I called to cancel the booking, they claimed 'we' had arrived earlier. Despite all the alarm bells raging, I decided there must have been a mistake. He texted me later to say his mother had been taken ill, and that he would make it up to me. My friend at the time was ready to drive to the hotel and confront him—in one of those sliding doors moments, I occasionally wonder if I would be in a different space now if we had.

My doubts, however, were further alleviated when, approximately six months into our relationship, he shared his dream of starting a construction company. He had construction expertise and my background was in accounting. He said we were the perfect team.

He presented the idea with such enthusiasm and conviction that I believed he genuinely wanted a future together.

Rapidly, without time to think, I became involved in the business venture; my substantial financial investments were made, office space was leased, company vehicles and machinery were acquired, and substantial loans were secured by me, primarily due to his alleged financial entanglements with his ex-partner.

The excitement reminiscent of our early weeks returned, propelling me back into the whirlwind of this new phase.

It was peculiar, I felt like an addict. The highs were amazing, the lows unbearable.

This second pass of the whirlwind was more intense than the first—

we had a business together now, and the whirlwind buffered me around in all of my people-pleasing glory. It didn't leave me time to question the bits in that whirlwind that would periodically smack me in the face or jab at me hard, just like debris picked up in a real whirlwind.

The issues in this relationship were intermittent but constant, like deflecting thrown objects. Someone would occasionally call the office asking for a different woman, then apologize for their mistake. We once received a speeding fine for his car from a location hundreds of miles away from where he said he was for work.

The ferocity of this whirlwind didn't leave me time to dwell on the reasons that his phone was so often broken so I couldn't reach him, or why when it wasn't he always took it into the bathroom when he took a shower.

Or why when we went out to dinner it was always miles away from our hometown.

The business grew quickly, as did the associated overheads—the value of the next car he would need, to see the calibre of high-net-worth clients we wanted to attract.

Soon without really noticing, I was working eighteen-hour days, spreading myself between building sites, quantity surveying and office tasks, while finding more than 20k a month to service the overheads, the cars mainly and he spent more and more time away in CEO mode, in nice hotels, securing jobs.

I was desperately unhappy and exhausted but pretending I wasn't, and my children hated him, as in their world I was absent a lot because of him, and I hated what I had allowed myself to become.

They deserved better; they didn't care that I drove a lovely car, or that the next deal was worth six figures or that I treated them to nice gifts to compensate; they did care that I wasn't there to play with them and that when I was, he was also there, reeking of expensive aftershave and talking about work.

But I kept on going through the motions. I had invested a lot in this venture, physically, financially and emotionally; failure was not an option.

And to add to my load, my very successful, well-respected businessman father had made it quite clear that he would disown me if the business went wrong. I also wanted to get this right to please my partner, so ultimately there would be more time and togetherness.

Two years of my life went by in this part of the perfect storm. Then in the late summer of 2008, the phone call came.

The faceless female voice telling me to do the decent thing and walk away from the business, and from her beloved, so she, his fiancé, could step into the role that was rightfully hers and they could finally be happy. My role! My business. The role I had created, invested heavily in in every conceivable way. She concluded her call by giving me a deadline, also telling me that I had better not put a scratch on the new car he had bought her; the car that my money had recently purchased for myself! That I was surprised he wanted to use it so often, when he had a Range Rover on the drive. My car, a beautiful white Mini Cooper.

It was one of those 'plot twist' moments in a movie. I was floored.

I thought then that was my life-defining moment. The one where I planned my exit strategy.

How naive was I?

Of course he had a really viable reason for the call. The fact that it was a random woman who had become obsessed with him since he had become so successful, and I was just to ignore it.

Even though I didn't want to believe that this was anything other than that, those gut feelings I had silenced for too long came back in stereo.

How had I been so stupid.

I withdrew, physically, emotionally and financially. I made it quite clear that I wasn't putting any more money into the business. What had I created?

Then one day in mid-October of that year, he calmly walked into the office and declared that I could stop having my tantrum now and start refocusing on the business and making us "some serious money again" as the woman who had called me was no longer a problem as she was dead.

I was sick; physically sick; I didn't know her, but in that moment, I knew that he did, and here was a reason for her calling me that day, and that reason could have only been she believed what she had told me was her truth. She had sadly taken her own life, leaving behind children from her earlier marriage.

And people love to talk, and the lies and deceits began to unravel. The obituaries in the local newspaper referred to her leaving her children and her fiancé behind.

This was the point I told him I was done, at which point he grabbed me by the throat, looked me in the eye and told me we were done when he said so. That was the first time in this whole series of horrific events I began to fear for my own safety.

The whirlwind was about to become a hurricane.

Hurricane Season

The weeks that followed that poor lady's death were hard. I was verbally abused by apparent strangers for my perceived part in it. I had abusive calls to my office number. I couldn't bear him to be in the same room as me. I was done with his lies, and I was scared for what was to come.

I began to make discoveries that only further solidified my need to walk away; jobs that I had been told were cancelled but had been paid to him in cash. Cheques that had been cashed but couldn't be accounted for. Things were further amplified, as people loved a scandal, and those people were falling over each other to share their whispering with me at every opportunity. Just as I thought things were as bad as they could get, our office was ransacked overnight.

I was scared and alone, with two children to protect, and the shame of what I felt was my own stupidity in all of this kept me from reaching out to anyone for support. And as the global credit crisis peaked, our contracts were being put on hold further adding to my pressure.

I suggested that we close the company, pay off our debts, go our separate ways and I could take back what was left, and we could both cut our losses on the rest.

He told me he would do the same as the lady who had claimed to be his fiancé if I forced him to do that, then that would be on my conscience too and pointed out how I always went out of my way to make him feel bad about himself.

Then came that fateful morning

I still remember that morning vividly, standing at the counter, staring at the attendant as each of my cards was declined one after another. My heart pounded and my hands shook as I realised what it meant—there was no money left. The weight of the situation crashed down on me, and in that moment of desperation, I had no choice but to call my dad.

With a lump in my throat, I dialled his number. Gladly he was always in his own office at that time of day. When he answered, I tried to keep my voice steady, but the panic was evident. I lied, telling him a half-baked story about a banking glitch, just to avoid the shame and embarrassment of the truth. He graciously agreed to cover the fuel, unaware of the storm that was raging in my life.

Trying to keep things as 'normal' as possible, having just lied to my dad so he would pay for my fuel, I dropped the children at school.

Just before arriving at school, my daughter, who we had always affectionately called 'spooky pookie' because she often came out with spooky yet accurate declarations like this, leant over and said to me, "he's not coming back Mum; he's gone".

This day was about to become my biggest, scariest life defining moment.

Not the day I got the telephone call from the fiancé, not the day he strolled into the office delivering news of someone's passing like he was talking about the weather.

But that day, 12th November 2008.

The day my life changed forever.

Still not fully recovered from the shame and embarrassment of my petrol-paying moment, the hurricane that was suddenly my life kicked up a notch, picking my life up with it to eventually spit out at some unknown location at some undetermined point in the future.

As the day progressed, the extent of the betrayal became apparent. My daughter was correct; he had disappeared, taking with him all the remaining funds in our bank accounts, credit cards, and the business. He had also declared bankruptcy, changed his contact information, and vanished. This left me and my two children to deal with the fallout that was inevitable.

He left us to face the other individuals he had scammed or not paid. He left me with the responsibility of explaining the situation to others. He abandoned us to face intimidating individuals demanding their money at our door. Furthermore, I was accused of being complicit in his actions and had to prove my own innocence rather than anyone seeking to prove his guilt.

In the span of time between leaving the office on the 11th and waking up on the 12th, I found myself with nothing. My sanity, mental health, and safety were precarious. It was now up to me and my two children to navigate this challenging situation alone.

~

In the following months, I lost my home and had to move quickly due to being stalked by others he had scammed. The phone abuse became unbearable, so I changed my number. I needed an emergency £100 loan from the welfare system to feed my children, which brought shame and verbal abuse at the welfare office. When that money ran out, I sold my possessions on eBay, which supported us for several months and helped me recover.

I had to give a statement to his official receiver and went under investigation as part of that.

I was even arrested and released without charge on an allegation made by one of his brothers.

My father kept his promise and kept his distance.

My friends didn't think I would ever recover.

Others were quick to tell me how stupid I had been and that I deserved everything I was experiencing.

I also discovered that I had tried to take out multiple loans in the days leading up to the 12th of November that had been declined, even though I hadn't.

It was a hard time to navigate.

I was taking whatever work I could find.

My most significant realisation during this time though was discovering myself and freedom.

Despite the challenges occurring behind the scenes, I needed to understand two core things:

- Why people treat others poorly for financial reasons.
- How I, a well-educated individual with a background in finance, had allowed this situation to occur and become so involved.

This marked the beginning of my journey of self-discovery.

The Calm After the Storm

I didn't know at this point that Money Mindset and early conditioning from your upbringing had such a profound impact on how you move through life.

Money Mindset was not a term that I had ever heard of.

While it is now evident that he moved through life using anyone he could to serve his own agenda where money was concerned, I was a perfect storm of vulnerable, newly single, and making good money. I later discovered that most of the ladies he had in his life—yes, there were several—were not dissimilar. Including the lady who sadly ended her life.

But despite this, and having the support of therapy, I needed to take complete responsibility for my part in it, the fact that I had allowed this to happen to me and my children.

It was the most challenging and rewarding journey I have ever undertaken. One of my core values is love. I was raised in an environment with conflicting sets of values and beliefs about money. As part of this upbringing, I learned to be a people pleaser to maintain peace.

Many years before my financial setback, I had unconsciously adopted behaviours that contributed to it. My mother instilled in me the belief that money needed to be earned through hard work; hence, my eighteen-hour workdays for the business. My father emphasized the importance of financial success for respect, which led to purchasing expensive cars, shoes, and other material items.

My grandparents' belief that discussing money was inappropriate created a sense of shame around failure and asking for help. My desire to be loved resulted in spending copious amounts of money on my partner and others to please them. My tendency to put others' needs and desires before my own further exacerbated the situation.

This combination of beliefs and conditioning formed an unconscious set of behaviours that I might never have recognized if not for this experience. It became clear to me that a poor relationship with and beliefs about money were widespread issues. This realisation marked the beginning of my work in this area.

Calmer Days

I needed to create something positive from my experiences, so I studied psychology, NLP, hypnotherapy, and other coaching modalities. With help from an amazing life coach, I started my coaching business. My goal is to help professional women achieve financial independence, remove societal vulnerabilities, and control their financial futures. Money can be a tough subject, especially for women, due to generational and societal biases. That was once me too. Since then, I have helped hundreds of women overcome their limits in money and business. My optimism, which helped me through childhood illness and heart surgeries, reminded me that neither those challenges nor a failed relationship could break me.

The Future

I dream of a world where women are financially empowered, free and independent. Who can talk openly and honestly to their own children, breaking the taboos around money and wealth, especially for women.

I am excited for women who love themselves and put their own needs first and are not afraid to ask for what they want and deserve and go after that with passion.

Initially, the shame of losing it all was harder than the actual loss.

But shame never solved any problem, and every day is a new opportunity.

Whatever your current experience, especially where money is concerned, it only need be temporary.

Within a year of that November, life was good again and has continued to grow and evolve since.

If I can use my painful experience to uplift, help, and support others, I am grateful for the experience and the path it ultimately took me down.

ABOUT THE AUTHOR

Vicki is a business and money coach who believes that nobody should be fearful of money.

She is absolutely passionate about equipping people to make more empowering decisions about their own money, now and in to the future.

Since her own financial downfall in 2008, she has made it her mission to help hundreds of established entrepreneurs and individuals to up-level their money mindset, build brilliant businesses & create sustainable future wealth.

Money is and probably always will be an omnipresent resource, and nobody should feel fear around it; It is her mission is to educate, inspire and empower as many people as possible to be free of fear with their money.

She works with clients worldwide, online and in person, via one-to-one coaching and consulting, workshops, talks and seminars.

- hello@vicki-o.com
- www.vicki-o.com
- https://www.linkedin.com/in/vicki-o

ABOUT THE PUBLISHER

Inspired World Publishing was founded by journalist-turned-PR strategist Dina Behrman. It publishes books from entrepreneurs, changemakers and business leaders with a story to tell and expertise to share.

As a PR strategist Dina works with entrepreneurs who want to stop being the internet's best kept secret, become the 'go to' expert and create a much bigger impact in the world by sharing their story and expertise in the press.

She launched her business following a decade working as a journalist. She's worked as a publicist for a number of industry leaders, and has also helped hundreds of entrepreneurs learn how to do their own PR. She's been featured in Forbes, Entrepreneur, Huff Post, The Guardian, BBC radio, amongst others.

- Find out more: www.dinabehrman.com

Printed in Great Britain
by Amazon

61479411R00087